the wide WORLD of trade

NCEE

National Council on Economic Education

National Council on Economic Education gratefully acknowledges the funding of this publication by the U.S. Department of Education under PR Grant Number R304A010003. Any opinions, findings, conclusions, or recommendations expressed in the publication are those of the authors and do not necessarily reflect the view of the U.S. Department of Education.

ISBN 1-56183-136-0

Authors

Sarapage McCorkle
Director, Center for Entrepreneurship and Economic Education
University of Missouri-St. Louis

Bonnie T. Meszaros
Associate Director, Center for Economic Education and Entrepreneurship
University of Delaware

Mary C. Suiter
Associate Director, Center for Entrepreneurship and Economic Education
University of Missouri-St. Louis

Michael Watts
Professor of Economics
Director, Center for Economic Education
Purdue University

Reviewers

The authors express their thanks to the following reviewers from the 2003 Training of Writers program. Their insights and advice were appreciated.

Tiffany Brocious Winchester, VA USA	Kathy Heyse Elkhart, IN USA	Rebecca Pfaffenberger Indianapolis, IN USA
Ruth Cookson Virginia Beach, VA USA	Iryna Lavruhina Minsk, Belarus	Istvan Ricz Budapest, Hungary
Sarah Culver Birmingham, AL USA	Jan Michalko Banicova, Slovakia	Joanna Stefaniak Gdansk, Poland
Gloria Dance Fort Wayne, IN USA	Theresa Modlich Colorado Springs, CO USA	Zoran Sumajstorcic Zagreb, Croatia
Irina Danikova Tula, Russia	Nada Moric Zagreb, Croatia	Alice Temnick Cave Creek, AZ USA
Kea Deppe Franklin, IN USA	Cynthia Myers-Gregory New Palestine, IN USA	Batima Tolebayeva Uralsk, Kazakhstan
Valentin Teodor Ghiata Bucharest, Romania	Ia Natsvlishvili Tblisi, Republic of Georgia	Zinaida Visotskaya Minsk, Belarus
Linda Haley Rogers, AR USA	Sherrie Oman Elkhart, IN USA	Lile Zakauskiene Vilnius, Lithuania

The authors also recognize the excellent work by the authors of the *International News Journal, Inc.* upon which this publication was based – Robert Reinke, Margit McGuire, and Diane Wilcox Reinke.

The Wide World of Trade represents a revision and enhancement of *The International News Journal, Inc.*, first published in 1992 by the Joint Council on Economic Education (now the National Council on Economic Education). *The Wide World of Trade* is composed of 11 standards-based lessons, several of which are revisions of the most popular economics lessons from *The International News Journal, Inc.* The new lessons are designed to provide the teacher with more active-learning experiences to enhance student understanding of international trade and finance. *The Wide World of Trade* is intended to provide a common curriculum for partnership programs between U.S. and international classrooms at the middle-school level. Students around the world can learn about their global neighbors, the benefits of voluntary trade, the basis for trade, and foreign currency markets.

The development of this publication was undertaken as part of the Cooperative Education Exchange Program funded by the United States Department of Education under PR Grant R304A010003. NCEE extends its deep appreciation to the Department of Education for its support of this program. In particular, Dr. Ram N. Singh, Senior Research Analyst, National Center for Education Research, Institute of Education Sciences, U.S. Department of Education, provided valuable advice and assistance. We are also grateful that the United States Congress had the foresight to realize the need for economic education in the emerging market economies and the vision to see how an international exchange program such as the CEEP could benefit U.S. teachers and students.

The National Council on Economic Education thanks the authors, drawn from NCEE's unique network of affiliated councils and centers, Sarapage McCorkle, Director of the Center for Entrepreneurship and Economic Education at the University of Missouri, St. Louis, who took the lead on the project; Bonnie Meszaros, Associate Director of the Center for Economic Education and Entrepreneurship at the University of Delaware; Mary Suiter, Associate Director of the Center for Entrepreneurship and Economic Education at the University of Missouri, St. Louis; and Michael Watts, Director of the Center for Economic Education at Purdue University.

Robert F. Duvall, Ph.D.
President and CEO
National Council on Economic Education

The Wide World of Trade is a set of eleven lessons that teach middle-school students about international trade and finance. The lessons are stand-alone, allowing teachers to select the lessons that best fit their students. Several lessons are based on the most popular lessons in the *International News Journal, Inc.* published in 1992 by the Joint Council on Economic Education, now known as the National Council on Economic Education (NCEE). Because global neighbors have become increasingly interdependent, it is commonplace to hear or read about international trade, trade restrictions, and how weak or strong the dollar is relative to other currencies. Unfortunately, most people know less about these international trade topics than they know about economics in general. The lessons in this publication are designed to teach students basic knowledge and principles about international trade and finance and to provide more insight into how the world of international trade works.

The Wide World Trade incorporates features that we think will make the lessons successful in middle-school classrooms. Some of those features are highlighted below.

- International trade and finance lessons – the lessons teach concepts such as scarcity, resources, opportunity cost, voluntary exchange, specialization and trade, comparative advantage, interdependence, gross domestic product, standard of living, exports, imports, trade barriers, foreign currency, and foreign currency markets

- Standards-based economics lessons – each lesson has been correlated to the national voluntary content standards in economics. See pages vii – ix for specific content standards and benchmarks for each lesson.

- Active learning approaches – each lesson includes hands-on activities. These active approaches were included because they are usually more effective in motivating students. These activities also provide a point of reference for teachers to use in later lessons and discussions. Many activities require students to get up and move in the classroom as they simulate some real-world process. There are many opportunities for discussion and group work. However, there is also opportunity for independent work. Every lesson includes visuals and/or graphic organizers.

- Integrated Curriculum – each lesson integrates language arts (reading, writing, oral communication). Several lessons integrate geography (maps, physical geography) and several integrate math (data analysis, computation, estimation, charts, tables).

- Assessment – all lessons include suggested assessments. Assessments include multiple choice questions, short response items, or extended response items. The short and extended response items require students to use the economic understanding to analyze, synthesize, or evaluate.

We hope that *The Wide World of Trade* will be used by middle-school teachers in the United States to enhance student understanding of important issues, such as the benefits of trade, the basis for trade, trade barriers, and foreign currency markets. We also hope that *The Wide World of Trade* will provide a common curriculum for partnership programs between U.S. and international classrooms at the middle-school level. As a result, students around the world can learn about their global neighbors while gaining important economic understanding.

Sarapage McCorkle, University of Missouri-St. Louis
Bonnie Meszaros, University of Delaware
Mary C. Suiter, University of Missouri-St. Louis
Michael Watts, Purdue University

Content Standard 1

Productive resources are limited. Therefore, people cannot have all the goods and services they want; as a result, they must choose some things and give up others.

↓ Benchmarks / Lessons →	1	2	3	4	5	6	7	8	9	10	11
People make choices because they cannot have everything they want.	X										
The opportunity cost of a choice is the value of the best alternative given up.	X	X					X				
Scarcity is the condition of not being able to have all of the goods and services one wants. It exists because human wants for goods and services exceed the quantity of goods and services that can be produced using all available resources.	X										
Like individuals, governments and societies experience scarcity because human wants exceed what can be made from all available resources.	X										
Productive resources are the natural resources, human resources, and capital goods available to make goods and services.	X		X								
Natural resources, such as land, are "gifts of nature;" they are present without human intervention.	X				X						
Human resources are the quantity and quality of human effort directed toward producing goods and services.	X				X						
Capital goods are goods produced and used to make other goods and services.	X				X						
Human capital refers to the quality of labor resources, which can be improved through investments in education, training, and health.					X						
Choices involve trading off the expected value of one opportunity against the expected value of its best alternative.							X				

Content Standard 5

Voluntary exchange occurs only when all participating parties expect to gain. This is true for trade among individuals or organizations within a nation, and among individuals or organizations in different nations.

↓ Benchmarks / Lessons →	1	2	3	4	5	6	7	8	9	10	11
Exchange is trading goods and services with people for other goods and services or money.		X	X			X	X				
People voluntarily exchange goods and services because they expect to be better off.		X	X			X	X				
When people buy something, they value it more than whatever it costs them; when people sell something, they value it less than the payment they receive.						X					
Free trade increases worldwide material standards of living.				X				X	X		

↓ Benchmarks / Lessons →	1	2	3	4	5	6	7	8	9	10	11
Despite the mutual benefits from trade among people in different countries, many nations employ trade barriers to restrict free trade for national defense reasons or because some companies and workers are hurt by free trade.								X	X		
Imports are foreign goods and services purchased from sellers in other nations.						X		X			X
Exports are domestic goods and services sold to buyers in other nations.						X		X			X
Voluntary exchange among people or organizations in different countries gives people a broader range of choices in buying goods and services.			X	X		X					

Content Standard 6

When individuals, regions, and nations specialize in what they can produce at the lowest cost and then trade with others, both production and consumption increase.

↓ Benchmarks / Lessons →	1	2	3	4	5	6	7	8	9	10	11
Greater specialization leads to increased interdependence among producers and consumers.			X								
Specialization and division of labor usually increase the productivity of workers.		X					X				
Like trade among individuals with one country, international trade promotes specialization and division of labor and increases output and consumption.						X	X	X			
As a result of growing international economic interdependence, economic conditions and policies in one nation increasingly affect economic conditions and policies in other nations.									X		
Two factors that prompt international trade are international differences in the availability of productive resources and differences in relative prices.		X									
Individuals and nations have a comparative advantage in the production of goods and services if they can produce a product at a lower opportunity cost than other individuals or nations.							X				

Content Standard 7

Markets exist when buyers and sellers interact. This interaction determines market prices and thereby allocates scarce goods and services.

↓ Benchmarks / Lessons →	1	2	3	4	5	6	7	8	9	10	11
A market exists whenever buyers and sellers exchange goods and services.											X
Most people both produce and consume. As producers they make goods and services; as consumers they use goods and services.											X

↓ Benchmarks / Lessons →	1	2	3	4	5	6	7	8	9	10	11
Market prices are determined through the buying and selling decisions made by buyers and sellers.											X
An exchange rate is the price of one nation's currency in terms of another nation's currency. Like other prices, exchange rates are determined by the forces of supply and demand. Foreign exchange markets allocate international currencies.										X	X

Content Standard 11

Money makes it easier to trade, borrow, save, invest, and compare the value of goods and services.

↓ Benchmarks / Lessons →	1	2	3	4	5	6	7	8	9	10	11
Most countries create their own currency for use as money.										X	

Content Standard 15

Investment in factories, machinery, new technology, and the health, education, and training of people can raise future standards of living.

	1	2	3	4	5	6	7	8	9	10	11
Workers can improve their productivity by improving their human capital.					X						
Standards of living increase as the productivity of labor improves.					X		X				

Content Standard 17

Costs of government policies sometimes exceed benefits. This may occur because of incentives facing voters, government officials, and government employees, because of actions by special interest groups that can impose costs on the general public, or because social goals other than economic efficiency are being pursued.

	1	2	3	4	5	6	7	8	9	10	11
Incentives exist for political leaders to implement policies that disperse costs widely over large groups of people and benefit relatively small, politically powerful groups of people.									X		

Content Standard 18

A nation's overall levels of income, employment, and prices are determined by the interaction of spending and production decisions made by all households, firms, government agencies, and others in the economy.

	1	2	3	4	5	6	7	8	9	10	11
Gross Domestic Product (GDP) is a basic measure of a nation's economic output and income. It is the total market value, measured in dollars, of all final goods and services produced in an economy in one year.					X						
Per capita GDP is GDP divided by the number of people living in a country.					X						

LESSON DESCRIPTION

Working in groups that represent countries, students randomly draw cards from boxes labeled natural resources, human resources, and capital goods. The groups use their available resources to provide for their citizens by satisfying their wants for food, clothing, housing, medical care, education, and entertainment for one year. The task is complicated when some countries learn that their resources are inadequate to produce as much as they had originally planned. No one country is able to satisfy all wants, so it must make choices. Students generate ways countries might deal with their scarcity problems.

ECONOMIC CONCEPTS

Natural resources
Capital goods (capital resources)
Human resources
Scarcity
Opportunity cost

OBJECTIVES – Students will:

- Define natural resources, human resources, capital goods, scarcity, and opportunity cost.
- Describe how the quantity and quality of productive resources vary among countries.
- Explain how scarcity of productive resources affects the amount of goods and services a country can produce.
- List ways a country might deal with the problem of scarce resources.

TIME REQUIRED

One to two class periods

MATERIALS

- Three shoeboxes labeled natural resources, human resources, and capital goods
- One copy of Activity 1.1, resource cards cut apart, placed in appropriate shoeboxes
- One copy of Activity 1.2 for each group
- Transparency of Activity 1.2
- Transparency of Visual 1.1
- One copy of Activity 1.3 for each student

PROCEDURE

1. Explain that in every country people must produce goods and services to survive. Productive resources are used to produce these goods and services. Define **productive resources** as the

natural resources, human resources, and capital goods available to make goods and services.

2. Tell students that **natural resources** are gifts of nature–things found in or on the earth. Ask for examples of natural resources. (*Answers might include rivers, minerals, animals, or plants.*)

3. Define **human resources** as the amount and quality of human effort used to produce goods and services. Ask students for examples of human resources. (*Answers might include teacher, mechanic, doctor, or truck driver.*)

4. Point out that human resources have skills, talents, and education; that is, they have **human capital**. Ask for examples of students' human capital. (*Answers might include computer, reading, writing, and math skills; talents in music, sports, or acting; ability to follow directions, serve as a group leader, and cooperate with group members.*)

5. Explain that **capital goods** are goods produced and used to make other goods and services. These include tools, equipment, and buildings. Point out that sometimes capital goods are called capital resources. Ask for examples of capital goods that are used in the classroom or school. (*Answers might include desks, books, school building, chairs, and computers.*)

6. Inform students that they will work in groups. Each group will represent a country. Divide students into groups of three. Give each group a copy of Activity 1.2. Have each group name its country and record the name on Activity 1.2.

7. Display the three productive resource boxes. Have a representative from each country draw a card from each box – natural resources, human resources, and capital goods.

8. Tell the groups to record the amount of each type of resource their country has in the spaces provided on Activity 1.2. Explain that the three drawn cards represent all the productive resources available for each country to use in the production of goods and services.

9. Inform students that they must use these resource amounts to produce food, clothing, housing, education, medical care, and entertainment for the citizens of their country. Each country has a population consisting of ten families.

10. Display a visual of Activity 1.2. Point out how many natural resources, human resources, and capital goods are needed to produce each of the goods and services necessary to survive. For example, food for one family requires: 10 natural resources,

10 human resources, and 10 capital goods. Food for ten families would require 100 units of each resource.

11. Tell students to decide how many units of food, clothing, housing, medical care, education, and entertainment they will provide and the number of natural resources, human resources, and capital goods used to produce each.

12. After each group has decided how to allocate its country's resources, draw the group's attention to its resource cards. Point out that some cards have a star. This indicates that the resources are of poor quality or not easily accessible. Countries with resource cards that have a star must reduce the amount of that resource by 25 units. For example, if a country has 450 units of human resources, it now has 425 units.

13. Allow students time to rearrange their allocation of resources to meet their wants of food, clothing, housing, education, medical care, and entertainment.

14. Have each country state its name and report how many of each type of resource it has. Record their responses on Visual 1.1. Discuss the following.

    a. Which countries are rich in natural resources? (*Answers will vary.*) Human resources? (*Answers will vary.*) Capital goods? (*Answers will vary.*)
    b. Are some countries richer in all three types of resources? (*Yes.*) Which ones? (*Answers will vary.*) What does a higher number of resources mean for families in these countries? (*Families are able to satisfy more wants.*)
    c. Are families in some countries able to satisfy most of their wants? (*Yes.*) Explain why. (*Some countries have more resources and resources of better quality than others.*)
    d. Are there countries in which families are able to satisfy only a few of their wants? (*Yes.*) Explain why. (*These countries have few resources, resources of poor quality, or resources that are not easy to access.*)

15. Point out that in this activity the amount of productive resources available varies greatly from country to country. Tell students that this holds true for countries around the world. Some countries, such as Russia, are rich in natural resources; some countries, such as the USA, have superior capital goods; and some countries, such as India, have large numbers of human resources with excellent skills and knowledge.

16. Are people in any country able to satisfy all their wants? (*No.*) Why not? (*There aren't enough productive resources to satisfy all wants of the citizens for one year.*)

17. Tell students that this problem of not having enough resources to satisfy all wants is called **scarcity**. It is a problem that exists for individuals, businesses, and countries and can never be eliminated.

18. Ask how people in each country dealt with the scarcity of resources. (*People in each country had to make decisions about how many units of food, clothing, housing, education, medical care, and entertainment to produce. Some may have decided not to satisfy some wants. Some probably produced enough for some families and not enough for others. Some may produce enough for all families but not enough for the entire year.*)

19. Explain that every decision involves an opportunity cost. Define **opportunity cost** as the value of the best alternative given up. For example, students usually spend one hour after school doing homework and one hour with friends. If students need to study for a test, they may give up time with their friends. Their opportunity cost is time with friends. In the case of the countries, the opportunity cost is the next best choice of how to use resources.

20. Ask students what their opportunity costs were for the decisions they made to allocate their productive resources. (*Answers will vary. One example might be some medical care given up in order to produce more food. The opportunity cost of producing more food would be some medical care.*)

21. Which countries had resource cards with stars? (*Answers will vary.*) How did the reduction in resources affect the ability of people in the country to meet their wants? (*They were able to satisfy even fewer wants than they originally had planned.*)

22. What might cause a reduction in the availability of quality of each type of resource? (*human resources – fewer people able to work, workers with poor skills, and lack of knowledge or capital goods; natural resources – located in places that are too costly to access or lack of capital goods to harvest the natural resources; capital goods – lack of technology and modern tools, machines, and other equipment*)

23. Tell students that people must decide how to deal with scarcity because it can never be eliminated. Ask how people in a country might satisfy more wants. (*find ways to increase the amount of goods and services produced using existing resources; produce what they can and trade for what they don't have*)

24. Point out that, in fact, people try to find ways to produce more goods and services of better quality with the given resources. They specialize and produce those things they can produce best. Then they trade resources, goods, and services that they have for those that they don't.

CLOSURE

Review the key points of the lesson using the following discussion questions.

1. What are productive resources? (*the natural resources, human resources, and capital goods available to make goods and services*)

2. What are natural resources? (*gifts of nature, things found on or in the earth*) Give an example of a natural resource. (*Answers will vary but might include minerals, trees, soil, and animals.*)

3. What are human resources? (*the quantity and quality of human effort used to produce goods and services*) Give an example of a human resource. (*Answers will vary but will include examples of various workers.*)

4. What is human capital? (*the skills, talents, education, and abilities that human resources possess*) Give an example of human capital. (*computer, reading, writing, and math skills; talents in music, sports, or acting; ability to follow directions, serve as a group leader, and cooperate with group members*)

5. What are capital goods? (*goods produced and used to make other goods and services*) Give an example of a capital good. (*Answers will vary but might include examples of various types of tools, factories, and machines.*)

6. Why is it difficult for people in a country to produce enough goods and services to satisfy all their wants? (*No country has enough productive resources; resources are scarce.*)

7. What does scarcity mean? (*Scarcity is the condition of not being able to have all the goods and services wanted. This is true for individuals, governments, societies, and countries.*)

8. Why does scarcity exist? (*Human wants for goods and services exceed the quantity of goods and services that can be produced using all available resources.*)

9. How does the scarcity of resources affect countries? (*They are unable to produce enough goods and services to satisfy all their citizens' wants such as food, clothing, housing, education, recreation, and medical care.*)

10. Why is there a wide range in the number of wants different countries can satisfy? (*Their resources vary greatly in amounts and quality.*)

11. How do the quantity and quality of a country's resources affect the quality of life of its citizens? (*Citizens in countries with poor resource endowments may have higher death rates, less educated population, high poverty rates, problems with hunger.*)

12. How might countries attempt to increase the number of goods and services they produce for their citizens? (*find ways to increase the amount produced given their existing resources; specialize in producing some goods and then trade for goods, services, and resources they do not have*)

ASSESSMENT

Distribute a copy of Activity 1.3 to each student. Instruct students to read the information about Countries A and B and complete the task.

EXTENSION

Teach "What, How, and For Whom to Produce?" from *Roosters to Robots: Lesson Plans from Writers around the World*," National Council on Economic Education.

★ 460 natural	★ 460 human	★ 460 capital
450 natural	★ 450 human	450 capital
★ 430 natural	430 human	★ 430 capital
400 natural	★ 400 human	400 capital
380 natural	380 human	★ 380 capital
380 natural	380 human	★ 380 capital
380 natural	380 human	380 capital
360 natural	360 human	360 capital
330 natural	330 human	330 capital

Country Name _____

Record the number of each type of resource your country has in the chart below.

NATURAL	HUMAN	CAPITAL

Resources Needed to Produce Each Good or Service
Per Family for One Year
(There are ten families in your country.)

Good or Service	Natural Resources	Human Resources	Capital Goods
Food	10	10	10
Clothing	10	10	10
Housing	10	10	10
Medical Care	5	5	5
Education	5	5	5
Entertainment	5	5	5

Country Decision on Number of Goods and Services to Provide

Good or Service	Number Produced	Natural Resources Needed	Human Resources Needed	Capital Goods Needed
Food				
Clothing				
Housing				
Medical Care				
Education				
Entertainment				

Read the description for each country and answer the questions that follow.

Country A

Country A is a small country with a large population. It has few natural resources and little land available for farming. It has a highly educated population and many skilled workers with access to the latest technology. Country A tries to satisfy the wants of its citizens by using its productive resources to produce goods and services.

Country B

Country B is a large country with a large population. It has many natural resources, including many acres of fertile land. Its workforce is large but has access to few quality capital goods and technology. Most of Country B's people have less than an 8th grade education. Country B tries to satisfy the wants of its citizens by using its productive resources to produce goods and services.

Task: Select one country and complete the following.

1. Describe the scarcity problem that people in this country face.

2. Explain how this scarcity problem affects the ability of people in this country to satisfy their wants.

3. List one way that people in this country might be able to deal with the scarcity problem.

Country Name	Natural Resources	Human Resources	Capital Resources

LESSON DESCRIPTION

Pairs of students play the roles of two friends who have chores to complete before they can spend time together. Through trial-and-error, students discover the benefits of specialization and trade. A second activity identifies reasons why people, businesses, and countries gain by specializing in the production of some goods and services.

ECONOMIC CONCEPTS

Exchange (trade)
Specialization

OBJECTIVES – Students will:

- Define specialization and trade (exchange).
- Evaluate the benefits of trade between individuals.
- Explain that people in different regions of the same country or people in different countries benefit from trade.
- Explain that specialization reduces costs and increases the variety of products available.

TIME REQUIRED

Two to three class periods

MATERIALS

- One copy of Activities 2.1, 2.2, and 2.3 for each student
- Transparency of Activity 2.2

PROCEDURE
Day One

1. Divide the class into pairs. If there is an extra student, let that student help distribute materials and record information on the board or overhead, or partner with the student.

2. Explain that in this activity each pair represents two friends. One person in each group will take the role of Marty. The second person may choose a name and take the role of Marty's friend, the narrator of the story.

3. Have the students choose their roles/names, then distribute a copy of Activity 2.1 to each student. Allow time for the students to read the story, or read it to the class.

4. Distribute a copy of Activity 2.2 to each student and display a transparency of Activity 2.2. Discuss the following.

    a. Suppose that you and your friend decide to split the tasks so that you weed 5 flowerbeds and wash 5 windows and Marty washes 5 windows and weeds 5 flowerbeds.

    b. Tell students that this is option "1." Have them write the number of flowerbeds weeded under column (2). Enter those numbers on the transparency for Marty and his friend. (5 for Marty and 5 for his friend)

    c. Have students calculate the number of minutes required to weed flowerbeds by multiplying the amount in column (2) by the number of minutes required to weed for each person. Record their answers in column (3) on the transparency and tell students to record their answers. (*100 minutes for Marty's friend and 250 minutes for Marty*)

    d. Have students repeat steps (B) and (C) for the minutes required to wash windows in column (5). Write the answers on the visual. (*50 minutes for Marty's friend and 100 minutes for Marty*)

    e. Tell students to add the total minutes required to weed gardens and wash windows for Marty and for his friend. (*150 minutes for the friend; 350 minutes for Marty*)

    f. Ask if weeding and window washing were divided this way, how long would it take? (*It would take 350 minutes.*) Explain that the friend would be finished in just 150 minutes, but the task would not be completed until Marty finishes. So, this strategy would lead to a finishing time of 350 minutes.

5. Tell pairs to try other strategies (options), such as 4 flowerbeds and 6 windows or 6 flowerbeds and 4 windows. For each strategy, they should complete another row on their worksheets. Help them with the math where needed.

6. Have the pairs report on the fastest strategy that they were able to find. (*Most pairs should have discovered that the fastest strategy is to have the friend weed all ten flowerbeds and have Marty wash all ten windows. Each would require 200 minutes to complete their individual tasks, so the pair would complete all work in 200 minutes.*)

7. Explain that doing just one of these two jobs is an example of **specialization**, which in general terms means producing a few things even though you buy and consume many more things. When people specialize they must exchange (trade) for other goods and services that they want but don't produce. **Trade** is exchanging goods and services with people for other goods and services or for money. Discuss the following.

    a. Who should specialize in weeding flowerbeds? (*the friend*)

    b. Who should specialize in washing windows? (*Marty*)

    c. If Marty specialized in washing windows, how would he get his flowerbeds weeded? (*He'd have to trade with his friend.*)

d. If Marty and his friend had specialized in the other product, how much time would have been required? (*It would take the friend 100 minutes to wash 10 windows. It would take Marty 500 minutes to weed 10 flowerbeds. Thus, the partners would finish all work in 500 minutes.*)

e. Do Marty and his friend minimize the amount of time they work by specializing either way? (*No, the amount of time is minimized when Marty specializes in washing windows and his friend specializes in weeding flowerbeds.*)

f. How do Marty and his friend benefit from specialization and trade? (*All work gets done in less time. Marty and his friend have more leisure time, so they are both better off.*)

8. Summarize that that when Marty and his friend specialize and trade, they're able to produce a given amount of clean windows and weeded flowerbeds in the shortest amount of time. This means they both have more time to do other things and they are better off.

Day 2

1. Remind students about the choices Marty and his friend made by discussing the following.

   a. What jobs were Marty and his friend assigned by their parents? (*washing windows and weeding flowerbeds*)

   b. How were Marty and his friend better off as a result of specialization and trade? (*They had the work completed in less time, so they had more leisure time.*)

2. Explain that people and businesses in different countries specialize and trade, too. They do this because they expect to "do better" or be better off as a result. Just as Marty and his friend were better off after they specialized and traded.

3. Distribute a copy of Activity 2.3. Tell students that the next discussion will help identify reasons why people and businesses in countries benefit by specializing in the production of some goods and services. Tell students that you will discuss five major points about specialization. Students should fill in the blanks in the appropriate box each time you make a new point. Then they should write one important idea that they hear during your discussion. Discuss box "A" as an example, and then discuss the following.

   A. *Even if you are good at making everything, it doesn't pay to do everything for yourself because you could be better off with specialization and trade.*

♦ As we saw with Marty and his friend, people and businesses specialize and trade.
♦ People and businesses in different countries are better off when they specialize and trade.
♦ People and businesses usually buy the things that cost them more to produce from other people and businesses, including people and businesses in other countries.
♦ Industrialized nations like the United Sates often buy things from other countries that they could make or even did make at one time. For example, it now costs less to import shoes than it would to move workers and other resources out of the production of some other good or service and into the production of shoes.

B. *Some people have special abilities and some countries have resources that others do not have. This leads to some specialization.*

♦ Marty's friend had a special tool to help him weed.
♦ Similarly, some counties produce oil or diamonds because of special "gifts of nature" that other countries don't have. Other countries may grow agricultural crops because of fertile land and good climates.
♦ Countries with a good business climate for capital investments tend to specialize in manufacturing.
♦ Countries with highly trained and skilled workers produce more "high tech" goods and services such as computers, airplanes, medical tools and supplies, architecture and engineering services, etc. This helps to explain why countries that are different trade with each other.

C. *Even when people and businesses in countries are similar – that is, they start out with the same or similar abilities and resources – it doesn't make sense for a person or business in a country to try to produce everything.*

♦ An important reason for this is that, over time, specialization makes people better at producing some things than other things.
♦ At first, Marty and his friend had little experience and training in weeding and washing windows. Over time, if they specialized so that only one of them washes windows and only one weeds, they are likely to become better at the job because they do it over and over again. Getting better could mean doing a better job or doing the job faster or both.
♦ The same things happen when businesses specialize: car companies learn more and more about designing, building, and selling cars, while computer companies learn about computers.

♦ Eventually with experience, training and specialized tools and machines people become better at producing their product than most other people; that is, the people produce a better product, faster.

D. *Specialization often leads to the development of tools and machinery designed to do one small part of producing a product, which might then be done hundred or thousands of times.*

♦ As we saw with Marty's friend, when people use tools they can do things better and faster.
♦ The development of special tools for specific parts of production increases production even more. If Marty and his friend decided to start washing windows and weeding flower beds for other people in the neighborhood in order to earn income, they might decide to invest in more tools so they could do their jobs better and faster.

E. *People, businesses, and countries specialize in a particular product within an industry.*

♦ Fast food restaurants specialize in fast food. They don't compete with gourmet restaurants. As a result both fast food and gourmet food is available for consumers.
♦ A doctor may specialize as a pediatrician or a heart surgeon. As a result, there are more types of doctors available to treat particular people or particular illnesses.
♦ A business in one country may specialize in the production of small, fuel-efficient cars. A business in another country may specialize in the production of luxury cars. If a country imports some kinds of cars and exports others, the variety of car models available to consumers is increased.

4. Summarize that specialization leads to better and faster production and lower costs of production. This means that more goods and services are produced, and that consumers get the goods and services at lower prices than they would if the production was done where costs of production are higher.

5. Emphasize the idea that specialization leads to trade and that trade among nations occurs for exactly the same reason that people in the same city or nation trade – people expect to be better off. Point out that consumers also benefit because there's a greater variety of goods and services and different styles of goods and services.

CLOSURE

Review the key points of the lesson using the following discussion questions.

1. What is specialization? (*producing a few things even though you buy and consume many more things*)

2. What are the benefits of specialization and trade between two people like Marty and his friend? (*They are able to finish all the work in less time and have more time for other things.*)

3. What are some benefits of specialization for people and businesses in the same and other countries? (*greater variety of products, products at lower costs and lower prices, people have more time for other things.*)

ASSESSMENT

Have students make a list of ten things that they or their families consumed in the last week. Then have them put a check next to any of the ten items they listed that were produced by someone in the family. By show of hand, estimate the average number of checks on the lists for all students in the class. The number should be much less than ten.

Ask students to explain, orally or in writing, how difficult it would have been for the family to produce all ten items, whether the family would be better off or worse off if it tried to produce everything on this list, and why. Then ask students to explain what they or their parents traded to get the goods and services on the list that they did not produce for themselves. Ask students to explain why people specialize, and how that benefits both individual workers and the overall level of production in a country.

Note: A parent who is a doctor specializes in providing medical care. The parent earns income for his/her work and uses the income to buy goods and services that he/she doesn't produce for him/herself, such as automobile repair and food.

EXTENSION

Have students make a list of ten things their family uses that were produced in another country. Discuss what it would take to produce those goods and services in this country instead. In particular, if resources were used to produce these products, what kinds of things currently produced in this country would have to be given up, or purchased from other countries instead?

Part I

Your family just moved to a new city because your parents found new and better jobs. You have to admit the extra money they are earning is nice because they bought you a new bike and let you use the new computer one hour every evening to play your favorite CD games – "Mad Marvin's Garden and Amusement Park" and "Ruler of the Universe."

The bad thing about this is your parents are busier than ever at work, and now so are you because they say you are "old enough to be helpful." In other words, they tell you to start helping out more around the house. They give you two new "chores" to do every week. You must weed the flowerbeds and you must wash some windows.

The best thing about living in your new neighborhood is that you have made a new friend, Marty. Marty lives across the street. Marty's parents are pretty cool for old people, except that they talk way too much with your parents about "good ideas for things for the kids to do." They gave Marty the same chores to do every week that you got stuck with.

The whole thing was clearly a plot because when your parents told you about these jobs and you complained by saying Marty didn't have to do stuff like this, your parents just smiled and told you to ask Marty about it tomorrow. It turns out Marty was being told about his new chores at the exact same time you were told about yours. Definitely a plot.

The first week it took you 20 minutes to weed each flowerbed because you were able to use a special weeding tool that your father had. Marty spent 50 minutes weeding each bed. It took Marty 20 minutes to wash a window. It took you 10 minutes.

When your parents ask you how the first week of doing new chores went, you see your big chance. You try to sound exhausted when you tell them how much time it took, and that the worst thing was you didn't get to spend much time with Marty. You hope they will let you quit working, but instead they say that you and Marty should figure out a way to do things more quickly so that you'll have time to spend together.

"How can we do that?" you ask. Your parents say that you and Marty could probably figure out a way to trade jobs. "Trade? What do you mean?" you ask. Your parents smile and hand you the table below, and say that Marty is getting the same table tonight from his parents. You knew all along it was a plot.

You and Marty figured out that each week you must wash 10 windows and weed 10 flowerbeds. You talk it over and decide that your parents meant that the two of you could trade some window washing for weeding. You decide that the best trades would be ones that allow you and Marty to finish the work in the least amount of time. That way, you'll have more time to hang out and do fun stuff.

Talk this over with your friend and complete the tables on the next page to decide on the best strategy. Be ready to share your answers with your teacher and the rest of the class.

Marty's Friend's Options

(1) Option number	(2) Number of flowerbeds weeded	(3) Total minutes to weed a flowerbed (2) X 20	(4) Number of windows washed	(5) Total minutes to wash windows (4) X 10	(6) Total minutes required (3) + (5)
1					
2					
3					
4					
5					
6					
7					
8					

Marty's Options

(1) Option number	(2) Number of flowerbeds weeded	(3) Total minutes to weed a flowerbed (2) X 50	(4) Number of windows washed	(5) Total minutes to wash windows (4) X 20	(6) Total minutes required (3) + (5)
1					
2					
3					
4					
5					
6					
7					
8					

A. Even if you are good at making everything, it doesn't pay to do everything yourself because you might be better off with ____**specialization**_____ and trade.

People and businesses in different countries are better off when they specialize and trade.

B. Some people have _____ abilities, and some countries have _____ that others do not.

Why do people and countries make some things, but not everything?

C. Even when people and countries start out with the same abilities and resources, it doesn't make _____ for a person or a country to try to produce everything.

D. Specialization often leads to the development of _____ and _____ designed to do one small part of producing a product.

E. People and businesses specialize in a particular _____ within an _____.

LESSON DESCRIPTION

In this lesson, students learn about resources from around the world that are used in the production of a specific product – Hershey's Kisses. Students then determine the identity of a mystery product using clues about world resources that are used to produce it. In both activities, students use world maps to identify trade flow patterns. Through the activities, they learn about economic interdependence and the benefits of trade. The second activity is based on a famous article written by Leonard E. Read in 1958, *I, Pencil: My Family Tree as Told to Leonard E. Read.*

ECONOMIC CONCEPTS

Productive resources
Exchange
Specialization
Interdependence
Benefits of trade

OBJECTIVES – Students will:

- Define productive resources, exchange, and specialization.
- Describe the consequences of exchange (trade).
- Explain the benefits of specialization and trade.

TIME REQUIRED

Two class periods

MATERIALS

- Hershey's Kisses (optional)
- One copy of Activity 3.1
- One copy of Activity 3.2 for each student (two pages)
- One copy of Activity 3.3 for each student (two pages)
- One copy of Activity 3.4, cut apart
- Student atlases (one for each student or group)
  A world map is available at
  http://www.cia.gov/cia/publications/mapspub/maps/World_Map_2.htm
- Wall world map
- Small sticky notes, yarn, scissors, transparent tape
- Small prizes (Hershey's Kisses or some non-candy product)

PROCEDURE
Day One

1. Write "Hershey's Kisses" on the board (or give a "Kiss" to each student), asking how many students have eaten them. Point out that Hershey's Kisses are familiar, but students probably haven't thought about how Hershey's Kisses came to be, the ingredients used, where the ingredients are found, and how the Kisses are made.

2. Explain that you will read a story about Hershey's Kisses. Tell the students to write down the productive resources that they hear listed in the story, explaining that **productive resources** are the natural resources (gifts of nature), human resources (people's work), and capital goods (goods produced and used over and over to make other goods and services) that are available for production. (See Lesson 1 for more on resources.) Tell the students to listen also for the countries in which people buy Hershey's Kisses.

3. Read the story of Hershey's Kisses on Activity 3.1. Ask which productive resources were described in the story. (*cocoa beans, milk, sugar, aluminum foil, paper, workers, machines*)

4. Give a copy of both pages of Activity 3.2 to each student and distribute scissors and paper. Tell students to cut, match, and tape the dashed lines. Point out the illustrations of resources used to produce Hershey's Kisses at the bottom of the map. Below each illustration and resource name is a list of major world producers. Explain the following.

    ♦ Cocoa beans: They are produced from cocoa trees in these countries.
    ♦ Sugar: It is produced from sugar cane from these countries.
    ♦ Aluminum: Essential resources for producing aluminum foil are located in these countries.
    ♦ Wood pulp: Wood pulp to produce the paper plume comes from trees in these countries.

5. Tell students to locate the countries on the map and draw the symbol for that product on the appropriate countries. Students should draw a line from the countries that provide resources to Hershey, Pennsylvania. Then students should draw a line from Hershey, Pennsylvania to the countries mentioned in the story in which Hershey's Kisses are bought, other than the USA. (*Mexico, Japan, Hong Kong, Taiwan, People's Republic of China, Puerto Rico, Guam, Thailand, Malaysia, Indonesia, Saudi Arabia, Canada*)

6. Explain that many exchanges occur in this case study. **Exchange** is trading goods and services with people for other goods and services or money. Hershey Foods Corporation buys resources from people in other countries; people in other countries buy Hershey's Kisses.

7. Point out that world trade (exchange) makes it possible for chocolate products, as well as other products requiring resources not found in the United States, to be produced in the

United States. Without world trade, production of such products might not be possible.

8. Explain that people benefit from world trade because voluntary exchange among people or organizations in different countries gives them a broader range of choices in buying goods and services. Because the United States is located more than 20 degrees above the equator, it would be extremely difficult to grow cocoa beans.

Day Two

1. Remind students about the Hershey's Kisses case study. Tell them that they will study about world trade involved in another product. From clues, students will identify a mystery product.

2. Give each student a copy of Activity 3.3 (both pages) and distribute scissors and tape. Tell students to follow the directions to create a world map.

3. Explain that students will receive cards that give resource clues to the identity of the mystery product. The cards will be read aloud.

4. Give a clue card from Activity 3.4 and two sticky notes to each student in class. If there are more than 24 students in class, appoint some students as helpers. (Helpers should receive only one sticky note.) Explain that each reader will read the card number and the clue when it's his or her turn. Each reader should also write the number and name of the resource (noted in italics on each card) on the sticky note. Allow time for the readers to write the information. Note: Students might ask for an explanation of some resources such as ammonium hydroxide. Explain that they may research these items later. Detailed explanations are not provided because the students must work at guessing the mystery product.

5. Explain that students will use these numbers on their personal maps. If a single location is mentioned and there is no movement of a resource involved, they should write only a number at an appropriate point on the world map. If the clue indicates movement of a resource, they should draw a line from place to place at the appropriate locations on their maps and number the line. For reference purposes, give a student atlas to each student. If you don't have enough atlases, divide the class into small groups and give an atlas to each group.

6. Explain that you (and any helpers) will work on the world map on the wall. You will place the sticky note related to each clue card on the map at the appropriate location, and you will string a piece of yarn from one location to another, when appropriate.

Tell students to write the name of the mystery product whenever they think they've solved the mystery on their second sticky note and put it on a designated spot on the classroom wall. Tell them to write their name and mystery product solution on the "sticky" side of the note, so that they can put it on the wall and no one will be able to see their answers.

7. Model the process as follows.

   ♦ Put a sticky note in eastern Tennessee with "mystery product factory" written on it, explaining this is the location where the mystery product is produced. (A pushpin will be useful.)
   ♦ Have the appropriate student read Card #1. Tell students to find Oregon on their maps and write "1." Place the sticky note in the appropriate place on the wall map.
   ♦ Have a student read Card #2. Put the sticky note on Malaysia on the wall map. Have students write "2" on Malaysia on their maps.
   ♦ String a piece of yarn from Malaysia to Tennessee. Tell students to draw a line from #2 to #1 on their maps.
   ♦ Explain that this is the process that they will follow.

8. Have students continue reading cards. Continue placing their sticky notes on the wall map. The rest of the class will continue to draw on their individual maps. Continue stringing yarn from one location to another, where appropriate.

9. After the class has completed the activity, ask the following. As the class answers each question, write the answers on the board with each answer directly under the previous.

   a. Which resource was produced in Italy? (*pumice*)
   b. What does the TVA produce for the mystery-product factory? (*electricity*)
   c. Where is candelilla wax produced? (*New York*)
   d. Which resource comes from Mississippi? (*clay*)
   e. Which Oregon tree is used to produce the mystery product? (*Incense-cedar*)
   f. What is the machine that paints the mystery product? (*lacquering machine*)

10. Explain that you will now "produce" the mystery product, using an acronym. Describe an acronym as a word formed from the initial letters of a series of words. The first letters of the answers are p, e, n, c, i, and l, or pencil. The mystery product is a pencil. See how many students answered correctly and give each a small prize. (Note: Some students may wonder what the plug is. It's the eraser. Some may wonder what a ferrule is. It's the metal band that covers the joining of the wood and the plug.)

11. Have students look at the world map and the wall map. Point out that it took a lot of resources from many places in the world to make a simple pencil. See if they can think of more resources used to make a pencil. (*railroad cars and tracks for shipping, ships for ocean shipping, people who produce each of the resources, factories, and so on*)

12. Point out that the Tennessee pencil factory (fictitious in this activity) depends on many producers of resources who, in turn, depend on many others. **Specialization** occurs when people, businesses, and organizations concentrate their production on fewer kinds of goods and services than they consume. Ask for examples of products/ resources in which businesses specialize in this mystery-product activity. (*Incense-cedar wood blocks, microchips, truck transportation, zinc, copper, brass, machines, and so on*)

13. Explain that specialization provides people with a wider range of goods and services, but it also leads to interdependence among people. That is, people must rely on others for goods, services, and resources. Ask how many students and their families are self-sufficient, producing everything that they use. (*None-the fact that they are in school is proof.*) Point out that greater specialization leads to increased interdependence among producers and consumers. As shown in this activity and in the Hershey's Kisses activity, a benefit of world trade is that it gives people a broader range of choices in buying goods and services. If world trade didn't exist, people's choices would be restricted considerably.

14. Point out that people don't trade only goods or resources that they don't have in their regions. Zinc is produced in Missouri, and copper is produced in Utah. There are U.S. factories that use American zinc and copper to produce brass. Ask why a pencil factory might choose to buy Malaysian brass rather than American brass. (*Students are likely to respond that it is probably less expensive, which is a reasonable response.*)

15. Explain that the Malaysian brass producers are competing with the American brass producers. If Malaysian brass is less expensive than American brass and the quality is the same, the pencil producer may choose to use Malaysian brass to reduce the costs of production and keep the price of pencils lower.

16. Explain that competition among world sellers results in lower costs and prices, higher product quality, and better customer service.

CLOSURE

Review the key points of the lesson using the following questions.

1. What are productive resources? (*the natural resources, human resources, and capital goods available to make goods/services*)

2. What is exchange? (*trading goods and services with people for other goods and services or money*)

3. How do people benefit from world trade? (*They have a broader range of choices in buying goods and services.*)

4. Using examples from the lesson activities, give examples of goods and services in which people or organizations specialized. (*cocoa beans, aluminum foil, microchips, trucking services, pencils, zinc, lacquering machines*)

5. To what does specialization of production lead? (*interdependence*)

6. Why is economic interdependence a positive thing? (*People can't be self-sufficient. Specialization and trade provide people with a broader range of goods and services than would occur without them.*)

7. There are many automobile producers in the world. What does the competition among these producers generate? (*lower costs and prices, higher product quality, and better customer service*)

ASSESSMENT

1. In Mary's house, her dad does all the cooking and food shopping, her mother does all the cleaning, and the children help out whenever necessary. Who is specializing in production?

    a. Mom, Dad, and the children
    b. Mom and Dad *
    c. The children
    d. No one

2. Specialization and trade result in:

    a. Increased economic interdependence, higher costs, and more choices in goods and services.
    b. Decreased economic interdependence, lower costs, and self-sufficiency.
    c. Increased economic interdependence, lower costs, and more choices of goods and services. *
    d. Decreased economic interdependence, lower costs, and fewer choices of goods and services.

EXTENSION

1.	Have students go to related websites for more information on the following.

	♦	www.pencils.com (pencil production, renewable resources)
	♦	www.icco.org/menuqa.htm (cocoa and chocolate)
	♦	www.hersheys.com (Hershey Foods Corporation)

2.	Have students select another product and use a search engine on the Internet to find out which resources are used to produce the product. Students write a summary report and include a world map, showing the trade patterns involved in making the production of the product possible.

3.	Discuss or have students view the PBS video series, *Frontier House*, to determine what it would be like to be almost self-sufficient and have limited opportunities to specialize and trade.

4.	Teach Lesson 2, "Special Friends," from *The Wide World of Trade*.

5.	Teach Lesson 7, "Mutual (and Comparative) Advantage," from *The Wide World of Trade*.

The story of Hershey's Kisses begins with Milton S. Hershey, who owned a successful caramel factory in Lancaster, Pennsylvania. He studied the chocolate market and thought that the nation would enjoy chocolate confections. In the early 1900s, Hershey sold his caramel factory and built a chocolate factory. This was a good idea because many people bought and enjoyed his chocolate confections. In 1907, Hershey had another idea, which resulted in the invention of Hershey's Kisses made from milk chocolate.

Making the kisses starts with getting raw materials such as cocoa, sugar, and milk. Hershey located his factory in south central Pennsylvania to be near cows that produce the milk necessary to produce milk chocolate.

Another necessary ingredient in chocolate is cocoa beans. The cocoa tree grows only in the tropical areas within 20 degrees north or south of the Equator. Here the temperature, rainfall, and soil are perfect for cocoa trees to survive. Beneath the leaves of the cocoa tree are small flowers. When the flowers are fertilized, they yield fruit in ripened pods. Inside the pods are the cocoa beans from which chocolate is made. The cocoa beans are shipped to Hershey's factories from the cocoa-growing areas of the world.

When the raw materials reach the factory, workers, using knowledge and skills to operate machinery and equipment, produce the kisses. Converting cocoa beans to chocolate products is complex and involves several steps. The beans are first cleaned and then roasted in revolving cylinders. At precisely the right moment, they pass from the roaster and are quickly cooled. The beans are then conveyed to chambers where they are shattered into small pieces to separate the shells from the inside of the bean – the nib. The dry nibs, now ready for milling, have cocoa butter, the natural fat of the cocoa bean, locked in their cells. The milling process not only continually reduces the size of the nibs but it also releases more of the cocoa butter. This process produces the liquid, called chocolate liquor, from which all chocolate is made.

At this point, milk, and sugar are added to the mixture, which is dried and smashed into a powder. The mixture is not ready for the refining process. Cocoa butter is added in the next step called "conching." Conches are machines in which the chocolate is rubbed across a base of corrugated granite by heavy rollers. Milk chocolate requires a very long conching time – up to 72 hours. After conching, the chocolate is passed through large, steel rollers that make it smooth. Here, while cooling, the chocolate is dropped into Hershey's Kisses molds.

The candy is then machine-wrapped in aluminum foil with a paper plume added. Hershey makes more than 70 million kisses a day in its factories in Pennsylvania, California, and Canada. Hershey Chocolate Company is the world's largest producer of chocolate and cocoa products. Hershey's Kisses are consumed by millions of people around the world. You can buy the kisses in such places as Mexico, Japan, Hong Kong, Taiwan, People's Republic of China, Puerto Rico, Guam, Thailand, Malaysia, Indonesia, Saudi Arabia, Canada, and, of course, the United States of America.

These facts are from *The Story of Chocolate and Cocoa*, and www.hersheys.com, Hershey Foods Corporation. The wrapped kiss configuration, attached plume, and the words *Hershey's Kisses* are registered trademarks of Hershey Foods Corporation, Hershey, PA 17033 USA, and are used with permission.

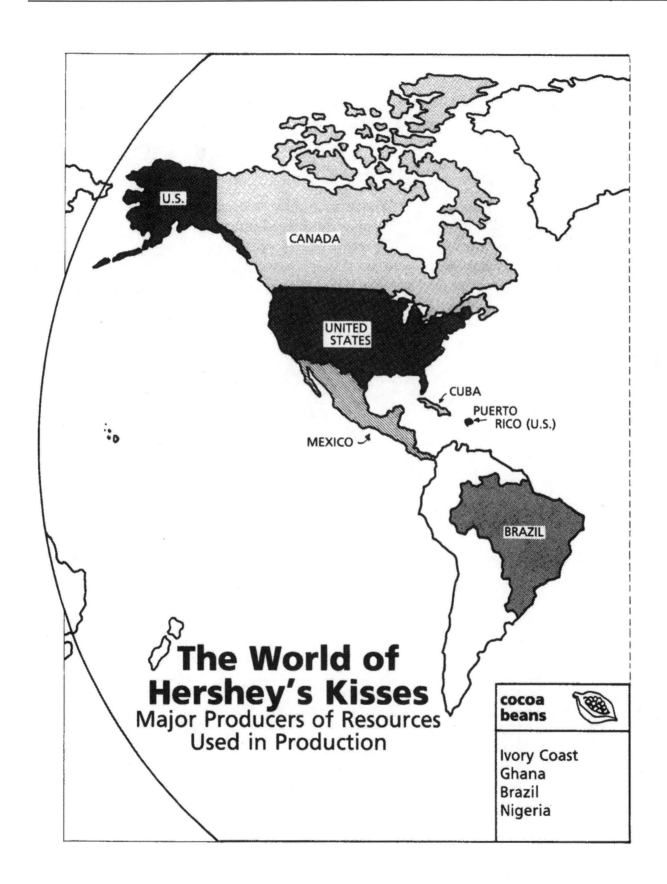

The World of Hershey's Kisses
Major Producers of Resources Used in Production

cocoa beans	
Ivory Coast	
Ghana	
Brazil	
Nigeria	

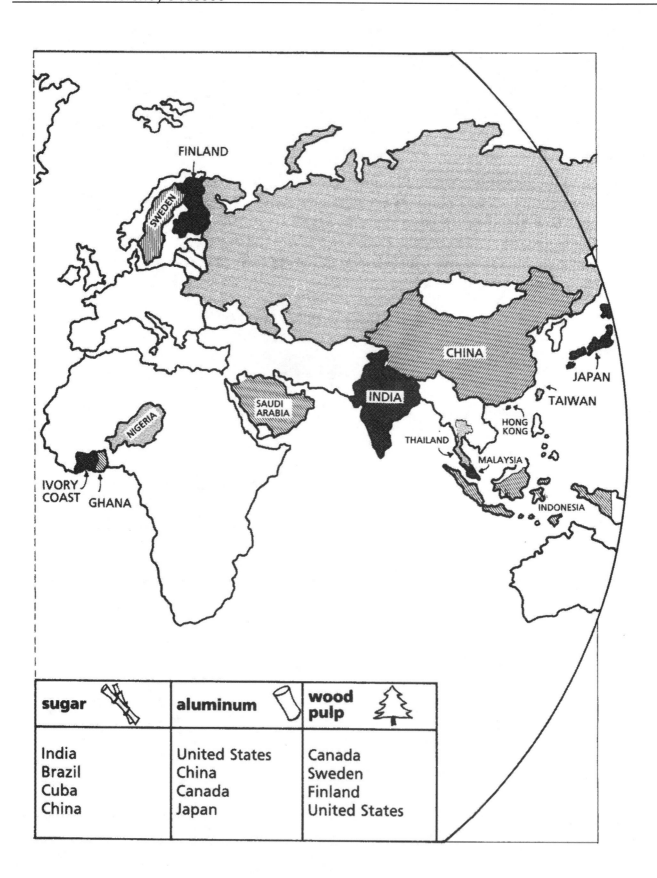

sugar 🍬	aluminum 🗑	wood pulp 🌲
India	United States	Canada
Brazil	China	Sweden
Cuba	Canada	Finland
China	Japan	United States

Cut along the dotted line of this portion of the world map. Match this page with the next page and tape to create a world map.

#1	#2
I am an *Incense-cedar tree* that grows in the Cascade Mountains of Oregon, USA. My smooth, fine grain and soft wood is ideal for making the mystery product. Loggers cut me down, and put me on a truck for shipping.	I am a *computer microchip* that was produced in Penang, Malaysia. I am used in a computerized milling process that cuts logs into wood blocks. I'm now doing my job at the Incense-cedar sawmill in the Cascade Mountains of Oregon.
#3	**#4**
I am a *Kenworth truck* that was built in Chillicothe, Ohio. I traveled across the country to Oregon. Then I traveled more and delivered the wood blocks to a factory in Tennessee.	I am a load of *Mississippi clay*. I am shipped from Mississippi to a factory in Tennessee where I am combined with other resources in a refining process to make part of the mystery product.
#5	**#6**
I am *graphite* from Sri Lanka. I am shipped to Tennessee to a factory where I am combined with other resources in a refining process.	I am a chemical compound called *ammonium hydroxide* that is produced in Georgia, U.S. I am mixed with graphite and clay in a refining process to make part of the mystery product.
#7	**#8**
I am a *cow* in Texas. After my demise, my processed fat will be combined with graphite, ammonium hydroxide, and clay in a refining process to make part of the mystery product.	I am the *candelilla plant*. I grow in northeastern Mexico in the foothills of the Chihuahua Mountains. I am shipped to New York where I am processed into wax.

#9	#10
I am *candelilla wax* that is made in New York. I am used to make cosmetics, polishes, pharmaceuticals, and chewing gum. I am also shipped to Tennessee to help make the mystery product.	I am *oil* that comes from Saudi Arabia which is in the Middle East, bordering the Persian Gulf and the Red Sea. Saudi Arabia has the largest proven petroleum reserves in the world. I am shipped to a refinery in Texas.
#11	**#12**
I am *paraffin wax* – a by-product from kerosene refined from petroleum. I was produced in Texas, and I am shipped to Tennessee to be mixed with candelilla wax to help make the mystery product.	I am a *Castor plant* that is native to Ethiopia in tropical east Africa. I am the key ingredient to producing castor oil. I am shipped to a factory in Massachusetts.
#13	**#14**
I am *castor oil*, and I am used to produce many products such as inks, lacquers, sealants, brake fluid, and soaps. Made in Massachusetts, I am shipped to Tennessee to help produce the mystery product.	I am *carbon black* that is produced in Italy and many other places. I am used as a pigment in printing inks. I am mixed with resins and applied by heat to the mystery product to make its label.
#15	**#16**
I am *zinc* that is mined in Australia. Did you know that zinc is the 23rd most abundant element in the earth's crust? I am shipped to a brass factory in Thailand.	I am *copper* that is mined in Kazakhstan. Kazakhstan is the world's 11th largest copper producer. I am shipped to a brass factory in Thailand.

#17	#18
I am *brass* made out of zinc and copper. I am manufactured in Thailand. I am stamped into a special shape and sent to a factory in Tennessee that uses me as the ferrule of the mystery product.	I am a *rapeseed plant* grown in Idaho. Canola and I are very similar. I am a genus of the mustard family, just like broccoli and brussels sprouts. I am used to make factice at the Tennessee plant.
#19	**#20**
I am a chemical compound called *sulfur chloride*. I am produced in India. I am used to make factice at the Tennessee plant for the mystery product.	I am *pumice* from Italy. Factice and I are used to make the "plug" for the mystery product at the Tennessee plant.
#21	**#22**
After the wood blocks are cut into wood slats and the wood slats are waxed and stained, it's my turn. I am a *grooving machine* that puts grooves into the slats so that a "core" can be put into the grooves. I was manufactured further west in Tennessee.	I'm a *slat press machine*. After the core is placed in the grooves, then another slat is put on top and I press the two slats together with the core in the middle, making a sandwich. I was also made further west in Tennessee.
#23	**#24**
The wood sandwiches are cut and shaped into long cylinders about 7" long. Sometimes the cylinders are round; sometimes they are hexagonal. Then they are painted in me, the *lacquering machine*. I was also built further west in Tennessee.	I am a *turbine* that was built in Germany. I generate electricity for the Tennessee Valley Authority (TVA) and I supply power to the mystery product's factory.

LESSON DESCRIPTION

Student groups represent people in different countries. Each group receives a packet of materials that represents productive resources. People in each country use the resources to provide food, clothing, shelter, businesses, and education. Because resources are unevenly distributed, people in the countries must trade in order to satisfy their wants.

ECONOMIC CONCEPTS

Voluntary exchange
Interdependence
Standard of living

OBJECTIVES – Students will:

- Explain how the quantity and quality of productive resources available in a country affects a country's ability to satisfy the wants of its people.
- Explain why people and organizations in countries trade.
- Explain how trade can improve the material standard of living of a country.
- Describe how trade creates interdependence.
- Explain how the restriction of a country's trading region limits the amount and quality of goods and services a country can provide for its people.

TIME REQUIRED

Two class periods

MATERIALS

- One copy of Activities 4.1 and 4.2 for each group
- Visual of Activity 4.2
- seven name tents (pieces of construction paper or poster board folded in half) labeled Country 1 – Country 7
- Large piece of chart paper
- seven markers, each a different color
- 10 paper clips
- 30 toothpicks
- two rulers
- two glue sticks
- four pencils
- four pairs of scissors
- 29 sheets of paper (8½" x 11" or 9" x 12") in the following colors-- 6 green, 5 red, 4 yellow, 7 white, 3 purple, 4 blue
- seven large manila envelopes for country packets prepared as follows.

> Country 1 – 1 sheet of green paper
>   3 sheets of yellow paper

Country 2 – 2 pairs of scissors
1 glue stick
2 pencils
1 ruler
1 sheet of red paper
Country 3 – 1 pair of scissors
1 glue stick
2 sheets of green paper
2 sheets of white paper
2 sheets of red paper
Country 4 – 1 ruler
2 pencils
2 sheets of purple paper
2 sheets of blue paper
2 sheets of white paper
Country 5 – 1 pair of scissors
30 toothpicks
2 sheets of white paper
1 sheet of red paper
Country 6 – 2 sheets of blue paper
2 sheets of green paper
10 paper clips
Country 7 – 1 sheet of green paper
1 sheet of yellow paper
1 sheet of white paper
1 sheet of red paper
1 sheet of purple paper

▪ One copy of Activity 4.3 for each student

PROCEDURE

1. Tell students that they will work in groups that represent different countries. They represent citizens of the country, and they must use the resources they are given to satisfy citizens' wants.

2. Divide students into seven groups as follows:
Country 1 – seven students
Country 2 – two students
Countries 3 through 7 – three to four students each

3. Give each group a name tent with the country's number on it.

4. Distribute manila envelopes to the appropriate countries. Tell students not to open the envelopes.

5. Explain that the envelopes contain a variety of materials that represent productive resources. Students will use these resources to produce goods and services to satisfy the wants of people living in the country.

6. Distribute a copy of Activity 4.1 to each group. Tell students that they must provide the food, clothing, shelter, businesses, and education people in the country want. Review the specifications for the patterns and models that must be used for production.

7. Inform students that the countries have different and unequal amounts of resources and, if they want, they may trade with other countries to obtain the resources they need.

8. Distribute a copy of Activity 4.2 to each group. Display a visual of Activity 4.2. Explain that each time a country's citizens make a trade, they must record what they gave up, what they gained, and the number of the country with which they traded. Review the example with the students.

9. Instruct each country to notify you when its citizens have completed production.

10. Allow time for students to produce. Provide enough time so all countries complete the task. Circulate among the groups to be sure that groups are only using materials provided in the seven country bags.

11. While students work in their groups, draw seven squares on a large sheet of chart paper. These squares should be randomly placed so that they form a circle or oval with one or two countries in the middle.

Sample Arrangement

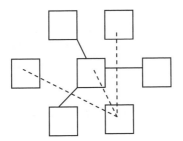

12. As each country finishes its task, ask one member to come to the board and use the information from Activity 4.2 to draw lines connecting its country with each of the other countries with which it traded. Provide each country representative with a different color marker.

13. When all countries are finished, discuss the following.

    a. Which countries had all the resources needed to satisfy their wants? (*none*) Point out that this a problem of scarcity. **Scarcity** means not having enough resources to satisfy everyone's wants.

b. Which resource was scarce for your country? (*Answers will vary. For example, countries 1 and 7 had no tools. Colored paper was scarce in Country 2. It only had red.*)

c. Which country had the most workers? (*Country 1*)

d. Which country was capital intensive; that is, it had many tools? (*Country 2*)

e. What decisions did you make because of scarcity? (*Students will mention that they decided to trade. They may mention the number of times they traded and how they used their resources.*)

f. Which resources did many people in many of the countries want? (*purple and red paper and scissors*) Why? (*Red and purple paper were necessary to provide education. Use of scissors made for better quality products.*)

14. Have representatives from each country show their products. Discuss the following.

a. In what ways do the products made in the various countries differ? (*Some have rough edges; some have smooth edges. Some are folded together, others are glued together, and others are held together with toothpicks. Some shelters are large with open sides; others are smaller with four closed sides, and so on. Some of the paper food is large and carefully shaped like the food it represents. Other paper food is small and only vaguely looks like the food it represents.*)

b. What might be a reason there was such wide variation in the way countries produced their final products? (*Answers will vary. There were differences in the quantity and quality of resources available, skills of workers, personal preferences, willingness to trade, and geography. Some countries may have tried to produce their products making as few trades as possible. Usually these countries have poor quality products. Show an example from one of these countries and an example from a country that made many trades. Some workers in a group may have lacked skills to construct the products. This, too, might have resulted in poorer quality goods. Show examples of these products. Other groups might have produced shelter based on geographic location and climate. A group might have produced an open-air tent because they determined that they lived in a climate that is warm year round. Show sample housing products.*)

15. Direct students' attention to the webs on the chart paper. Explain that voluntary exchange occurs when individuals or organizations voluntarily trade goods, services and resources for other goods, services and resources or for money. Discuss the following.

   a. Why did people in each country make multiple exchanges or trades? (*They did not have enough to satisfy their wants.*)

   b. How many trades did you make to satisfy your wants? (*Numbers will vary.*) How many countries did you trade with? (*Numbers will vary.*)

   c. Why did some countries make more trades than others? (*had more of one resource than they needed, but had fewer of other resources*)

   d. How many countries traded with country 4 or 7? (*All.*) Why? (*They were the only countries that had purple paper, which was needed to provide education.*)

   e. What might happen to your country's ability to provide education if these two countries refused to trade with your country? (*Quality might decline; less education would be available.*)

   f. Explain that people engage in voluntary exchange or trade because they expect to be better off. How did trade benefit people in your country? (*When we traded with people in other countries we were able to obtain enough resources to provide food, clothing, shelter, businesses, and education for its people.*)

   g. How did trade among people in different countries in the simulation create interdependence? (*People in different countries depended on one another for the resources needed to satisfy each other's wants.*) Point out that trade among individuals and organizations within and among countries include not only resources but also goods and services. Note: In the activity, some groups may have traded products for resources or products for products.

   h. How would the people in your country be affected if your trading region were restricted to include only the country closest to yours (the group closest to you)? (*People in the countries would not be able to satisfy all their wants.*) Ask students for specific examples of how this restriction would hurt people in their country. (*Answers will vary. Students should mention products they might have to do without or products that, if produced, would be of lesser quality. For example, if a country was not located next to country 4 or 7, it could not provide education or if a country needed scissors but was not located next to one that had scissors, its products would be of poorer quality.*)

16. Explain that a country's **standard of living** is determined by adding together the market value, measured in dollars, of all final goods and services produced in the country in one year and dividing that number by the population of the country. Point out that students don't know the dollar value of the total goods and services produced in each country in the simulation. However, based on the results of the simulation, students can make a generalization about how trade affects a country's standard of living. Discuss the following.

   a. What happened to your ability to provide goods and services for people in your country when you traded? (*increased*)

   b. How does trade affect a country's standard of living? (*Trade improves the country's standard of living. Through trade, there are more goods and services available for people in a country.*)

   c. Give an example of a country that has scarce resources, goods, and services, and its people must trade or find innovative ways to produce products. (*Answers will vary but could include any country.*)

CLOSURE

Review the key points of the lesson using the following discussion questions.

1. How is a country's ability to satisfy the wants of its people influenced by the quantity and quality of productive resources available in that country? (*Countries with few resources or resources of poor quality are not able to satisfy as many wants as countries with more and better quality resources.*)

2. Why do people and countries trade? (*They trade to be better off. They expect to obtain resources, goods, and services that they don't have.*)

3. How can trade improve the material standard of living of a country? (*By trading, people are able to produce and/or consume more goods and services to satisfy wants.*)

4. How might the differences in availability of productive resources influence trade among countries? (*Trade should increase in order to obtain the resources needed. This trade would make countries more interdependent.*)

5. How does limiting a country's trading region affect its people? (*It reduces the resources, goods and services available to its people.*)

6. How does trade create interdependence? (*People in different countries depend on one another for the resources, goods and services they do not have and cannot produce.*)

ASSESSMENT

Give a copy of Activity 4.3 to each student. Instruct them to read the scenario and answer the questions.

Suggested answers.

1. People in each school have something people in the other school want. If they trade, they expect to be better off. Madison will be able to play their home games on the same field, and Central will have an auditorium for its productions. Students at both schools are better off.

2. Like people in these schools, people and organizations from different countries trade because they expect to be better off. For example, in the simulation in class, our country traded our excess resources with a country that had resources we needed and that wanted what we had to trade. People in both countries were better off.

3. By trading the use of the school facilities, people in each school were depending on the other to provide something their students needed.

EXTENSION

Teach "Why Nations Trade," *Geography: Focus on Economics*, National Council on Economic Education, New York, NY, 1996.

You must produce food, clothing, shelter, businesses, and education in order to satisfy the wants of people in your country. All production must follow the specifications below.

1. **FOOD:** Produce patterns in the shape of three different kinds of food using three different colors, each color representing the actual color of the food.

2. **CLOTHING:** Produce a pattern for a piece of clothing that you might wear.

3. **SHELTER:** Produce a three-dimensional shelter, no smaller than 2" x 2" x 2".

4. **BUSINESSES:** Produce a four-link paper chain; each link must be a different color.

5. **EDUCATION:** Produce a four-page book. One page must be purple and one page must be red.

Country # _____

What was given up	Number of country with which you traded	What was gained
Piece of red paper	Country #3	Use of glue stick

Madison High School completed a new auditorium with air conditioning and state-of-the-art lighting and sound. Because of the cost of building this facility, no funds were allocated to maintain or upgrade the football field. The facility is so bad that officials have refused to officiate at Madison's home games for fear players will get injured.

Madison's rival, Central High School, has a beautiful new football stadium, but its auditorium has been condemned for fear that the ceiling will collapse. The School Board has allotted funds in next year's budget for renovating the auditorium. So, for this year, Central's music and drama departments will be without a facility to house their performances. Faculty, parents, administrators, and students at Central have proposed that Madison use Central's football stadium for Madison's six home games. In exchange, Central will use Madison's auditorium for its fall and spring school plays and concerts.

1. Why would people from these two schools be willing to make this trade?

2. How is this trade similar to trade between countries? Support your answer with an example using actual countries or those from the class simulation.

3. How does trading between people in different countries or between people from two different high schools create interdependence?

LESSON DESCRIPTION

Working in groups, students participate in an activity to identify
countries from around the world. Based on what they learn about
these countries, students complete an Information Resources Chart.
The goal is to have students recognize what information supplied
about the countries can tell them about the countries' resource
endowments and standards of living.

The source for the data used in this lesson is the *CIA World Fact
Book, 2002*found at www.odci.gov/cia/publications/factbook/

ECONOMIC CONCEPTS

Productive resources
Economic system
Natural resources
Human resources
Capital goods
Human capital and investment in human capital
Gross domestic product
Per capita gross domestic product

OBJECTIVES – Students will:

- Define natural and human resources, capital goods, human
  capital, and investment in human capital.
- Define gross domestic product and per capita GDP.
- Explain the relationship between investment in human capital and
  productivity.
- Explain that if there are more goods and services available per
  person in a country, the standard of living in that country
  improves.

TIME REQUIRED

Three class periods

MATERIALS

- One copy of Activity 5.1 for each student
- One copy of Activity 5.2 for each group (12 pages)
- One manila envelope or pocket folder for each group
- Transparency of Visual 5.1
- Four copies of Activity 5.3 for each student
- World map from textbook or atlas for each group
- World wall map
- One copy of Activity 5.4 for each student

PROCEDURE
Day One

1. Ask what detectives do. After several student responses, explain that detectives investigate and solve problems by gathering information and analyzing clues. Now, students will act as detectives. They will use clues and information they are given to identify mystery countries.

2. Explain that different countries around the world have different resources. **Productive resources** are the things used to produce goods and services. Different countries have different geographic characteristics that affect the types of resources the country has.

3. Distribute Activity 5.1 and tell students to use it for note taking. Point out that they will learn various terms to help them understand and interpret the information they will be given about the mystery countries. Discuss the following.

   a. Geography includes climate, geographic features, and land formations, such as mountains, plains, deserts, and bodies of water. Ask students to describe geographic features in their country or state. Have them identify something about the climate in their country or state.

   b. The handout students will receive has information about the country's economy. Every country has an economic system. An **economic system** (economy) is the way in which people, businesses, and governments interact as they decide how to use resources. The economy section includes information about industries found in countries. An industry is a group of businesses that provide similar products. For example, there are several automobile companies that make up the automobile industry in the United States. The economy section includes information about agriculture in the countries; that is, crops grown. Why is it valuable to have information about the economy in a country? (*It helps people know the type and variety of goods and services a country produces. It points out the valuable natural resources found in the country. It indicates what's available for trade.*)

   c. Each handout has information about phones, electricity, and transportation in a country. This information helps people understand something about how goods and services are produced in a country and about the quality of life.
      - Electricity tends to make people's lives easier. It is easier to produce food and other products using electricity. How does electricity make your life easier and better? (*heat, cooling, cooking food, light at night*). Note: Comparisons among countries regarding phones, electricity, and

transportation must take into account the population and size of the country.

- Communication allows people to share information more easily and it often makes it easier to educate people. Which communication methods do you use, and how do these improve your life? (*phone, television, computer, radio, newspapers, magazines; these provide information, education, and entertainment*)

d. Another piece of information provided about each country is per capita GDP. GDP stands for Gross Domestic Product. Gross means total. Domestic means within a particular country, and product means goods and services. **Gross Domestic Product** measures a nation's economic output; that is, it measures the total value of the nation's goods and services that are produced in some time period. It is the total market value of all final goods and services produced within a country's borders during some time period, usually a year.

- The GDP of an economy can be computed, but people must know the market value of the goods and services. Market value is computed by multiplying the number of goods and services by their prices.
- Capita means head or person. Per capita GDP is the amount of income available for each person in the country. If a country's GDP is $1,000 and the population is 500, what is its per capita GDP? ($2 = $1,000/500)
- It is useful to know the per capita GDP in a country because it gives us an idea about how many goods and services are available for each family in a country, on average. This tells us something about the standard of living in the country.

e. A piece of information provided about each country is the percentage of arable land. Arable land is land that is fit for growing crops. So this statistic tells people what part of all the land in a country is fit for growing crops. Why is it useful to know the percentage of arable land in a country? (*It helps people understand whether the country can grow many or few crops.*)

f. The information about each country includes the literacy rate. Literacy means the ability to read and write. The literacy rate tells what part or percentage of a country's entire population is able to read and write. Why is the literacy rate useful to know? (*It helps people understand the types of skills and education people living in a country have.*)

4. Divide the class into small groups, giving each group a world map. Distribute a copy of Activity 5.2 to each group. Tell students to use their notes, the clues in the handouts, and the world maps to identify each country. They should not share their answers with other groups. Allow time for students to work.

5.   Distribute a manila envelope or a pocket folder to each group. Tell students to write their names on the folder or envelope and place their handouts and answers in it. Collect the envelopes or folders.

Day 2

1.   Create two columns on the board. Title column one, "Mystery Country Number." Title column two, "Country Name." In column one, list numbers 1 through 12.

2.   Tell students to return to their groups from the previous class. Distribute the folders or envelopes to each group. If needed, allow time for groups to complete their work.

3.   Ask one member from one group to write the group's answers on the board in column two next to the number for each country.

4.   Tell other groups to compare their answers to the answers on the board. If a group has a different answer for a mystery country, a member from the group should go to the board and write that answer in column two, next to the answer already listed for that number. Have different groups explain on which information they based their decision for Mystery Country #1. (*Explanations will vary but may include land size, population, economic data, land formations or geographic features of the country.*) Repeat this process with the other mystery countries.

5.   Display Visual 5.1 with the correct answers for each mystery country. Point out that there may have been some information that led groups to select a different answer; however, all information combined limits the answer to the single country.

6.   Remind students that resources are the things used to produce goods and services. There are three broad categories of resources: natural resources, human resources, and capital goods (resources).

7.   Explain that **natural resources** are things found in or on the earth. They are "gifts of nature" that are present without human intervention. Trees, land, and minerals are examples of natural resources.

8.   Explain that **human resources** are the quantity and quality of human effort directed toward producing goods and services. Teachers, janitors, nurses, bus drivers, and mechanics are examples of human resources.

9.   Explain that **capital goods** (resources) are goods produced and used to make other goods and services. The school building,

desks, computers, overhead projectors, and televisions are examples of capital goods.

10. Explain that **human capital** refers to the skills, talents, and education that human resources have. Each student in the classroom has human capital. Students in the class can read, write, and compute. Some students may be musicians. Others may be volleyball players or dancers. All these skills and talents are part of the students' human capital. Ask for examples of human capital they possess. (*Answers will vary.*)

11. Explain that human capital can be improved through investments in education, training, and health care. For example, a student can improve knowledge by attending school, by reading, and by studying. A student can improve musical talent through practice.

12. Explain that people who have more education, who are healthier, and who have more skills and training have more human capital. People with more human capital are able to produce more and different types of goods and services than those with less human capital. Point out that students in seventh grade can produce many more school projects and different types of school projects than students in first grade. Children who have practiced piano diligently for hours each day will likely be able to play more complicated pieces than children who don't practice.

13. Explain that when people can produce more goods and services with the same amount of resources, productivity increases. Increased productivity can improve a country's standard of living. **Standard of living** is the level of goods and services people in a country have.

14. Have students work in their groups and identify information from the worksheets that might tell them something about the natural resources, human resources, and capital goods (resources) found in the countries, about the human capital people in the country possess, and about the country's standard of living. Discuss the following.

    a. What information might tell you something about the natural resources found in a country? (*percentage of arable land, land formations found in the country, climate of the country, information about the economy might include minerals found in the country*)
    b. What information might tell you something about the human resources found in a country? (*population, literacy rate, life expectancy*)
    c. What information might tell you something about the capital goods (resources) found in a country? (*information about*

the economy that is related to machinery, tools, and equipment; information about phones, transportation, and electricity available as compared to the population of the country)

    d. What information might tell you something about the human capital people in the country possess? (*literacy rates*)

    e. What information might tell you something about the standard of living in the country? (*per capita GDP*)

15. Tell students to return the handouts to their folders or envelopes. Collect the folders or envelopes.

Day 3

1. Explain that students will make some comparisons among the countries. Recording information about the countries in a chart will make it easier to read, compare, contrast, and discuss the countries.

2. Have students return to their groups. Distribute folders or envelopes to groups, and give four copies of Activity 5.3 to each student. Provide the following instructions.

    • Each row on Activity 5.3 is labeled with types of resource information.

    • Divide the Mystery Country handouts among the members of your group. Find and underline the required information on your Mystery Country handouts.

    • Group members should take turns reading the underlined information from their Mystery Country handouts to the rest of the group.

    • As group members read the information about a country, enter the name of the country in the first row. Record the reported information in the appropriate cell of the Resource Information Chart in the column for that country.

3. When groups have completed their work, discuss the following.

    a. How are all countries similar? (*All have natural and human resources and capital goods. All produce some goods and services.*)

    b. How do all countries differ? (*All are located in different places. They all have some different resources. The types of industries, crops, percentage of arable land, per capita GDP, and so forth, differ from country to country.*)

    c. Which country has the greatest percentage of arable land? (*Ukraine*) Lowest percentage of arable land? (*Egypt and Saudi Arabia both have 2%.*)

    d. How might the amount of arable land affect a country? (*If there isn't much arable land, people won't be able to grow as many crops. Also, some crops may grow better on less arable land than others. If there isn't much arable land, people may have to get food from other countries.*)

e. What country has the highest literacy rate? (*Australia*) Lowest literacy rate? (*Egypt*)

f. How might the literacy rate affect a country? (*Literacy rates tell us something about the human capital the people in a country possess. A high literacy rate indicates more human capital. People with more and better human capital should be able to produce more and different types of goods and services.*)

g. If a country has low literacy rates and few resources, will it be able to produce fewer or more goods and services compared to other countries with higher levels? (*fewer*)

h. In which countries do people grow rice? (*China, Egypt, Mexico, Peru*) Soybeans? (*United States, Mexico*) Coffee? (*Kenya, Mexico, Peru, Democratic Republic of the Congo*) Cotton? (*Egypt, Peru, United States, Mexico*) Vegetables? (*Egypt, United States, China, Ukraine*) Grains? (*Egypt, Australia, United States, Czech Republic, Mexico, China, Saudi Arabia, Ukraine, France*) Potatoes (*Czech Republic, France, China, Peru*) Sunflowers? (*Ukraine*) Sugarcane? (*Democratic Republic of the Congo, Kenya, Australia, Peru*) Tea? (*China, Kenya*)

i. Why do people in these countries produce these crops? (*People living in these countries or in other countries want these crops for food to eat or to make other products.*)

j. Which countries have petroleum (crude oil) resources? (*Saudi Arabia, Egypt, Australia, Mexico, Peru, Democratic Republic of the Congo, United States, Ukraine, China*) Gold? (*Democratic Republic of the Congo, Peru, United States, Kenya*) Tin? (*Australia, Democratic Republic of the Congo, China*) Iron ore? (*Egypt, Australia, Democratic Republic of the Congo, United States, Ukraine, France, China*) Bauxite? (*Australia, Democratic Republic of the Congo, United States, France*)

k. How might an abundance or lack of these resources affect the economic life of people in those countries? (*If there's an abundance of these resources, more goods and services could be produced for each person. People may be able to trade these resources or goods for other things they want but don't have in their country. If there's a lack of these resources the opposite is true.*)

l. In which countries do people produce electronic equipment? (*United States, France, China*) Chemicals? (*Saudi Arabia, Egypt, Australia, Mexico, United States, Ukraine, France, China*) Vehicles? (*Mexico, Peru, United States, Czech Republic, China*) Textiles? (*France, China, Kenya, Peru, Democratic Republic of the Congo, Mexico, Egypt*) Cement? (*Saudi Arabia, Egypt, Democratic Republic of the Congo, Peru, Kenya, China*) Refined petroleum? (*Saudi Arabia,*

United States, Kenya, China) Ships? (*Peru, France*)
Perfume? (*France*) Plastic? (*Kenya, United States*) Why
do people in these countries produce these things? (*People
living in that country or in other countries want these things.*)

m. If a country produces a lot of electronic equipment but has
little arable land, how could people obtain more food
products? (*trade with people in other countries who produce
food products and want electronic equipment*)

n. Which country has the highest per capita GDP? (*United
States*) Lowest per capita GDP? (*Democratic Republic of
the Congo*)

o. What does per capita GDP tell us? (*the amount of goods
and services available for each person in a country*)

p. If a country has a higher per capita GDP, what does that tell
us about the country's standard of living? (*It is higher.*)

Closure

Review the key points of the lesson using the following discussion
questions.

1. What are resources? (*things used to produce goods and
services*)

2. What are natural resources? (*things found in or on the earth,
gifts of nature*)

3. Give some examples of natural resources. (*oil, land, coal,
bauxite*)

4. What are human resources? (*the quantity and quality of human
effort directed toward producing goods and services*)

5. Give some examples of human resources. (*farmers, mechanics,
lawyers, teachers, truck drivers*)

6. What are capital goods? (*things made and used to produce
goods and services*)

7. Give some examples of capital goods used to bake cookies.
(*mixer, spoon, bowl, cookie sheets, oven*)

8. What type of resource is arable land? (*natural*)

9. What is human capital? (*the skills, talents, and education that
human resources have*)

10. If a country has a high literacy rate, what does it tell you about
the human capital people in the country possess? (*People are
able to read and write – they have some education.*)

11. If people in a country want to improve human capital, what can they do? (*provide more education and better health services*)

12. How does investment in human capital benefit a country? (*People with more and better human capital can produce more goods and services; more variety of goods and services can exist; and productivity can increase.*)

13. If productivity increased in a country and there were more goods and services available per person, what would happen to per capita GDP? (*rise*) Standard of living? (*improve*)

14. What is per capita GDP? (*Gross Domestic Product per person*)

15. What is gross domestic product? (*It is the total market value of all final goods and services produced within a country's borders during some time period, usually a year.*)

16. How is market value determined to calculate GDP? (*Market value is computed by multiplying the goods and services produced in the economy by their prices.*)

Assessment

Distribute Activity 5.4 to each student. Tell students to read the information about the country. Using the information provided and a world map, students should identify the country and answer the questions on the handout.

Extension

1. Have students visit the CIA World Factbook at www.odci.gov/cia/publications/factbook/ to learn more about the mystery countries and other countries.

2. Have students identify natural resources with which they are unfamiliar from the detective clue sheets. Then have students conduct research to find out what these resources are and what they can be used to produce.

3. If Lesson 4, "International Trade," from *The Wide World of Trade* was taught, have students explain why the country with an abundance of natural resources traded, why the country rich in capital goods traded, and how trade improved the standard of living in each country.

Please use this page to take notes about the terms you must understand to be a Mystery Country Detective.

Geography:

Economy:

Gross Domestic Product (GDP)/per capita GDP

Percentage of Arable Land

Literacy Rate

Clues for Mystery Country #1

People	♦ Population: 31,138,735
Economy	♦ Natural resources available include 569,250 square kilometers of land, gold, limestone, soda ash, salt barites, rubies, fluorspar, garnets, and wildlife. ♦ Seven percent of the land is arable. ♦ The per capita GDP in 2001 was approximately $1,000. ♦ Major industries include the production of plastic, furniture, batteries, textiles, soap, cigarettes, flour, petroleum refining, cement, and tourism. ♦ Agricultural products include coffee, tea, corn, wheat, sugarcane, fruit, vegetables, dairy products, beef, pork, poultry, and eggs.
Phones, Electricity, Transportation	♦ 310,000 phone lines in use; 540,000 mobile cellular phones in use – phone service is unreliable ♦ 4.433 billion kilowatts consumed ♦ 2,778 kilometers (km) of railways; 8,868 km of paved highway, 63,00 km of unpaved highway; 22 airports with paved runways.
Education	♦ Literacy rate: 78.1 percent of the total population over age 15 can read and write.
Geography	♦ There are 13,400 square kilometers of water. ♦ There are mountains in this country. ♦ Nearby countries include Tanzania, Ethiopia, and Somalia. ♦ The climate varies from tropical along the coast to arid in the interior. ♦ There are 536 kilometers of coastline. ♦ There is recurring drought in the northern and eastern regions of the country. There is flooding during the rainy season.
Health	♦ The life expectancy is 47 years.

Mystery Country #1 is _____

Clues for Mystery Country #2

People	♦ Population: 1,284,303,705
Economy	♦ Natural resources available include 9,326,410 square kilometers of land, coal, iron ore, petroleum, natural gas, mercury, tin, tungsten, antimony, manganese, molybdenum, vanadium, magnetite, aluminum, lead, zinc, and uranium. ♦ 13.31% of the land is arable. ♦ The per capita GDP in 2001 was approximately $4,300. ♦ Industries include iron and steel, coal, machine building, armaments, textiles and apparel, petroleum, cement, chemical fertilizers, footwear, toys, food processing, automobiles, consumer electronics, and telecommunications. ♦ Agricultural products include rice, wheat, potatoes, sorghum, peanuts, tea, millet, barley, cotton, oilseed, pork, and fish.
Phones, Electricity, Transportation	♦ 135 million phone lines in use; 65 million mobile cellular phones – phone service is increasingly more available for private use, unevenly distributed service (more for cities) ♦ 1.206 trillion kilowatts consumed ♦ 67,524 kilometers (km) of railways; 271,300 km of paved highways; 1,128,700 km of unpaved highways; 324 airports with paved runways.
Education	♦ Literacy rate: 81.5 percent of the total population over age 15 can read and write.
Geography	♦ There are 270,550 square kilometers of water. ♦ The terrain is mostly mountains and high plateaus. There are deserts in the west and plains, deltas, and hills in the east. ♦ Nearby countries include India, Pakistan, Afghanistan, and Kazakhstan. ♦ The climate is extremely diverse from tropical in the south to subarctic in the north. ♦ There are 14,500 kilometers of coastline. ♦ There are frequent typhoons along the southern and eastern coasts; damaging floods, tsunamis, earthquakes, and droughts.
Health	♦ The life expectancy is 72 years.

Mystery country #2 is_____

Clues for Mystery Country #3

People	◆ Population: 280,562,489
Economy	◆ Natural resources available include 9,158,960 square kilometers of land, coal, copper, lead, molybdenum, phosphates, uranium, bauxite, gold, iron, mercury, nickel, potash, silver, tungsten, zinc, petroleum, natural gas, timber. ◆ Nineteen percent of the land is arable. ◆ The per capita GDP in 2001 was approximately $36,300. ◆ Industries include crude oil production, petroleum refining, steel, motor vehicles, plastics, aerospace, telecommunications, chemicals, electronics, food processing, consumer goods, lumber, and mining. ◆ Agricultural products include wheat, other grains, soybeans, corn, fruits, vegetables, cotton, beef, pork, poultry, dairy products, forest products, and fish.
Phones, Electricity, Transportation	◆ 194 million phone lines in use; 69.2 million mobile cellular phones – very large, technically advanced system, reliable ◆ 3.613 trillion kilowatts consumed ◆ 212,433 Kilometers (km) of railways; 5,733,028 km paved highways; 637,003 km unpaved highways; 5,174 airports with paved runways
Education	◆ Literacy rate: 97 percent of the population 15 and over can read and write.
Geography	◆ There are 470,131 square kilometers of water. ◆ The terrain includes a vast central plain, mountains in the west and hills and low mountains in the east. ◆ Nearby countries include Cuba, Canada, and Mexico. ◆ The climate is mostly temperate. It is semiarid in the plains, and there are deserts. ◆ There are 19,924 kilometers of coastline. ◆ There are tsunamis, volcanoes, earthquakes, hurricanes, tornadoes, and flooding.
Health	◆ The life expectancy is 77 years.

Mystery country #3 is _____

Clues for Mystery Country #4

People	♦ Population: 59,765,983
Economy	♦ Natural resources available include 545,630 square kilometers of land, coal, iron ore, bauxite, zinc, potash, timber, and fish. ♦ Thirty-three percent of the land is arable. ♦ The per capita GDP in 2001 was approximately $25,400. ♦ Industries include machinery, chemicals, automobiles, metallurgy, aircraft, electronics, ships, textiles, food processing, wine, perfume and tourism. ♦ Agricultural products include wheat, cereals, sugar beets, potatoes, wine grapes, beef, dairy products, and fish.
Phones, Electricity, Transportation	♦ 34.86 million phone lines in use; 11.078 million mobile cellular – highly developed system, reliable ♦ 408.514 billion kilowatts consumed ♦ 31,939 kilometers (km) of railways; 892,900 km of paved highways, no unpaved highways; 268 airports with paved runways.
Education	♦ Literacy rate: 99 percent of the population 15 and over can read and write.
Geography	♦ There are 1,400 square kilometers of water. ♦ The terrain includes mostly flat plains or gently rolling hills in the north and the west. The remainder is mountainous. ♦ Nearby countries include Germany, Italy, and Spain. ♦ Most of the country experiences cool winters and mild summers. There are areas of mild winters and hot summers. ♦ There are 3,427 kilometers of coastline. ♦ There are floods and avalanches.
Health	♦ The life expectancy is 79 years.

Mystery country #4 is _____

Clues for Mystery Country #5

People	♦ Population: 103,400,165
Economy	♦ Natural resources available include 1,923,040 square kilometers of land, petroleum, silver, copper, gold, lead, zinc, natural gas, and timber.
	♦ Thirteen percent of the land is arable.
	♦ The per capita GDP in 2001 was approximately $9,000.
	♦ Industries include food and beverages, tobacco, chemicals, iron and steel, petroleum, mining, textiles, clothing, motor vehicles, and tourism.
	♦ Agricultural products include corn, wheat, soybeans, rice, beans, cotton, coffee, fruit, tomatoes, beef, poultry, dairy products, and wood products.
Phone, Electricity, Transportation	♦ 12.33 million main phone lines in use; 2.02 million mobile cellular —adequate service for business and government put the general population is poorly served
	♦ 182.829 billion kilowatts consumed
	♦ 18,000 kilometers (km) railways; 96,221 km of paved highways, 227,756 km of unpaved highways; 238 airports with paved runways.
Education	♦ Literacy rate: 90 percent of the population 15 and over can read and write.
Geography	♦ There are 49,510 square kilometers of water.
	♦ The terrain includes high, rugged mountains, low coastal plains, high plateaus, and desert.
	♦ Nearby countries include Guatemala, Belize, and Honduras.
	♦ The climate varies from tropical to desert.
	♦ There are 9,330 kilometers of coastline.
	♦ There are tsunamis, volcanoes, earthquakes, and hurricanes.
Health	♦ The life expectancy is 72 years.

Mystery country #5 is _____

Clues for Mystery Country #6

People	◆ Population: 70,712,345
Economy	◆ Natural resources available include 995,450 square kilometers of land, petroleum, natural gas, iron ore, phosphates, manganese, limestone, gypsum, talc, asbestos, lead, and zinc. ◆ Three percent of the land is arable. ◆ The per capita GDP in 2001 was approximately $3,700. ◆ Major industries include textiles, food processing, tourism, chemicals, hydrocarbons, construction, cement, and metals. ◆ Agricultural products include cotton, rice, corn, wheat, beans, fruits, vegetables, cattle, water buffalo, sheep, and goats.
Phones, Electricity, Transportation	◆ 3,971,500 phone lines in use; 380,000 mobile cellular phones in use – large system, reasonably modern and reliable ◆ 64.721 billion kilowatts consumed ◆ 4,955 kilometers (km) of railways; 50,000 km of paved highway, 14,000 km of unpaved highway; 69 airports with paved runways.
Education	◆ Literacy rate: 51.4 percent of the population 15 and over can read and write.
Geography	◆ There are 6,000 square kilometers of water. ◆ The terrain includes a vast desert plateau interrupted by a valley and a delta. ◆ Nearby countries include Libya, Israel, and Jordan. ◆ The climate is desert – hot dry summers with moderate winters. ◆ There are 2,450 kilometers of coastline. ◆ There are periodic droughts, frequent earthquakes, flash floods, dust storms and sandstorms.
Health	◆ The life expectancy is 64 years.

Mystery country #6 is _____

Clues for Mystery Country #7

People	◆ Population: 19,546,792
Economy	◆ Natural resources available include 7,617,930 square kilometers of land, bauxite, coal, iron ore, copper, tin, silver, uranium, nickel, tungsten, mineral sands, lead, zinc, diamonds, natural gas, and petroleum. ◆ Seven percent of the land is arable. ◆ The per capita GDP in 2001 was approximately $24,000. ◆ Industries include mining, industrial and transportation equipment, food processing, chemicals, and steel. ◆ Agricultural products include wheat, barley, sugarcane, fruits, cattle, sheep, and poultry.
Phones, Electricity, Transportation	◆ 10.05 million phone lines in use; 8.6 million mobile cellular phones in use – excellent service ◆ 188.489 billion kilowatts consumed ◆ 33,819 kilometers (km) railways; 353,331 km of paved highways, 559,669 km of unpaved highways; 271 airports with paved runways.
Education	◆ Literacy rate: 100 percent of the population 15 and over can read and write.
Geography	◆ There are 68,920 square kilometers of water. ◆ The terrain includes mostly low plateau with deserts and a fertile plain in the southeast. ◆ Nearby countries include Papua New Guinea and New Zealand. ◆ The climate is generally arid to semiarid. It is temperate in the south and east and tropical in the north. ◆ There are 25,760 kilometers of coastline. ◆ There are cyclones along the coast and severe droughts.
Health	◆ The life expectancy is 80 years.

Mystery country #7 is _____

Clues for Mystery Country #8

People	◆ Population: 55,225,478
Economy	◆ Natural resources available include 2,267,600 square kilometers of land, cobalt, copper, cadmium, petroleum, industrial and gem diamonds, gold, silver, zinc, manganese, tin, germanium, uranium, radium, bauxite, iron ore, coal, and timber.
	◆ Three percent of the land is arable.
	◆ The per capita GDP in 2001 was approximately $590.
	◆ Industries include mining of diamonds, copper and zinc; mineral processing; consumer products, such as textiles, footwear, processed food and beverages; and cement.
	◆ Agricultural products include coffee, sugar, palm oil, rubber, tea, quinine, cassava, palm oil, bananas, root crops, corn, fruits, and wood products.
Phones, Electricity, Transportation	◆ 21,000 phone lines in use; 15,000 mobile cellular phones in use
	◆ 4.55 billion kilowatts consumed
	◆ 5,138 kilometers (km) of railways; 157,000 km of highways – no information available regarding paved/unpaved; 24 airports with paved runways.
Education	◆ Literacy rate: 77 percent of the population 15 and over can read and write.
Geography	◆ There are 77,810 square kilometers of water.
	◆ The terrain includes a vast central basin that is a low-lying plateau and mountains in the east.
	◆ Nearby countries include Angola, Rwanda, Tanzania, and Zambia.
	◆ The climate is tropical; hot and humid in equatorial river basin; cooler and drier in southern highlands; and cooler and wetter in eastern highlands
	◆ There are 37 kilometers of coastline.
	◆ There are periodic droughts in the south, and there is some volcanic activity.
Health	◆ The life expectancy is 49 years.

Mystery country #8 is _____

Clues for Mystery Country #9

People	◆ Population: 27,949,639
Economy	◆ Natural resources available include 1,280,000 square kilometers of land, copper, silver, gold, petroleum, timber, fish, iron ore, coal, phosphate, and potash. ◆ Three percent of the land is arable. ◆ The per capita GDP in 2001 was approximately $4,800. ◆ Industries include mining of metals, petroleum, fishing, textiles, clothing, food processing, cement, auto assembly, steel, shipbuilding, and metal fabrication. ◆ Agricultural products include coffee, cotton, sugarcane, rice, wheat, potatoes, plantains, coca, poultry, beef, dairy products, wool, and fish.
Phone, Electricity, Transportation	◆ 1.509 million phone telephone lines in use; 504,995 mobile cellular phones in use – phone service is adequate for most requirements ◆ 18.301 billion kilowatts consumed ◆ 2,102 kilometers (km) of railways; 8,700 km of paved highway, 64,200 km of unpaved highway; 46 airports with paved runways.
Education	◆ Literacy rate: 88 percent of the population 15 and over can read and write.
Geography	◆ There are 5,220 square kilometers of water. ◆ The terrain includes a coastal plain in the wet, high and rugged mountains in the center, and lowland jungle in the east. ◆ Nearby countries include Ecuador, Bolivia, and Colombia. ◆ The climate varies from tropical in the east to dry desert in the west. The climate is temperate to frigid in the mountains. ◆ There are 2,414 kilometers of coastline. ◆ There are earthquakes, tsunamis, floods, and mild volcanic activity.
Health	◆ The life expectancy is 68 years.

Mystery country #9 is _____

Clues for Mystery Country #10

People	◆ Population: 23,513,330
Economy	◆ Natural resources available include 1,960,582 square kilometers of land, petroleum, natural gas, iron ore, gold, and copper. ◆ Two percent of the land is arable. ◆ The per capita GDP in 2001 was approximately $10,600. ◆ Industries include crude oil production, petroleum refining, basic petrochemicals, cement, construction, fertilizer, and plastics. ◆ Agricultural products include wheat, barley, tomatoes, melons, dates, citrus, mutton, chickens, eggs, and milk.
Phone, Electricity, Transportation	◆ 3.1 million phone lines in use; 1 million mobile cellular phones in use – modern phone system ◆ 114.86 billion kilowatts consumed. ◆ 1,392 kilometers (km) of railways; 44,104 km of paved highway; 102,420 km of unpaved highway; 70 airports with paved runways
Education	◆ Literacy rate: 78 percent of the population 15 and over can read and write.
Geography	◆ There are no square kilometers of water. ◆ The terrain is mostly uninhabited, sandy desert. ◆ Nearby countries include Jordan, Iran, and Syria. ◆ The climate is harsh, dry desert with great extremes in temperature. ◆ There are 2,640 kilometers of coastline. ◆ There are frequent sand and dust storms.
Health	◆ The life expectancy is 68 years.

Mystery country #10 is _____

Clues for Mystery Country #11

People	◆ Population: 10,256,760
Economy	◆ Natural resources available include 77,866 square kilometers of land, hard coal, soft coal, kaolin, clay, graphite, and timber. ◆ Forty-one percent of the land is arable. ◆ The per capita GDP in 2001 was approximately $14,400. ◆ Industries include metallurgy, machinery and equipment, motor vehicles, glass, and armaments. ◆ Agricultural products include wheat, potatoes, sugar beets, hops, fruit, pigs, and poultry.
Phone, Electricity, Transportation	◆ 3.869 million phone lines in use; 4.346 million mobile cellular phones – phone system is improving ◆ 54.701 billion kilowatts consumed ◆ 9,444 kilometers (km) of railways; 55,432 km of paved highway; no unpaved highway; 43 airports with paved runways
Education	◆ Literacy rate: 99 percent of the population 15 and over can read and write.
Geography	◆ There are 1,590 square kilometers of water. ◆ The terrain includes rolling plains, hills and plateaus surrounded by low mountains in the west and very hilly country in the east. ◆ Nearby countries include Germany, Slovakia, and Hungary. ◆ The climate is temperate; cool summers; cold, cloudy, and humid winters. ◆ There are no kilometers of coastline. ◆ There is flooding.
Health	◆ The life expectancy is 75 years.

Mystery country #11 is _____

Clues for Mystery Country #12

People	♦ Population: 48,396,470
Economy	♦ Natural resources available include 603,700 square kilometers of land, iron ore, coal, manganese, natural gas, oil, salt, sulfur, graphite, titanium, magnesium, kaolin, nickel, mercury, and timber. ♦ Fifty-seven percent of the land is arable. ♦ The per capita GDP in 2001 was approximately $4,200. ♦ Industries include coal, electric power, ferrous and nonferrous metals, machinery and transport equipment, chemicals and food processing. ♦ Agricultural products include grain, sugar beets, sunflower seeds, vegetables, beef, and milk.
Phone, Electricity, Transportation	♦ 9.45 million phone lines in use; 236,000 mobile cellular phones in use – system is improving ♦ 151.72 billion kilowatts consumed ♦ 22,510 kilometers (km) of railways; 236,400 km of paved highway; 37,300 km of unpaved highway; 114 airports with paved runways.
Education	♦ Literacy rate: 98 percent of the population 15 and over can read and write.
Geography	♦ There are no square kilometers of water. ♦ The terrain includes fertile plains and plateaus, with mountains in the west and in the extreme south. ♦ Nearby countries include Belarus, Slovakia, and Hungary. ♦ The climate is temperate continental. Precipitation is higher in the west and north and lower in the east and southeast. Winters vary from cool along the coast to cold further inland. Summers are warm across the greater part of the country and hot in the south. ♦ There are 2,782 kilometers of coastline.
Health	♦ The life expectancy is 66 years.

Mystery country #12 is _____

Data			
Natural Resource Information ♦ Natural Resources Found ♦ Percent of Arable Land ♦ Square Kilometers of Water			
Capital Goods Information ♦ Major Industries ♦ Phones ♦ Electrical Power ♦ Transportation			
Human Resource and Human Capital Information ♦ Literacy Rate ♦ Population ♦ Per Capita GDP			

Use the information in the table below, a world map from your textbook or an atlas, your Resource Information Charts for the other twelve mystery countries, and your human capital to answer the questions that follow the table.

People	♦ Population: 144,978,573
Economy	♦ Natural resources available include 16,995,800 square kilometers of land, oil, natural gas, coal, and strategic minerals, and timber. ♦ Eight percent of the land is arable. ♦ The per capita GDP in 2001 was approximately $8,300. ♦ Industries include mining and production of coal, oil, gas, chemicals, metals, machine building including aircraft and space vehicles, shipbuilding, road and rail transportation equipment, agricultural machinery, electric power equipment, medical and scientific instruments. ♦ Agricultural products include grain, sugar beets, sunflower seed, vegetables, fruits, beef, and milk.
Phones, Electricity, Transportation	♦ 30 million phone lines in use; 2.5 million mobile cellular phones in use – progress has been made but a large demand for main line services remains unmet ♦ 767.1 billion kilowatts consumed ♦ 87,157 kilometers (km) of railways; 752,000 km of paved highway; 200,000 km of unpaved highway; 471 airports with paved runways.
Education	♦ Literacy rate: 98 percent of the population 15 and over can read and write.
Geography	♦ There are 79,400 square kilometers of water. ♦ The terrain includes broad plains with low hills west of the mountains, vast coniferous forest and tundra, and uplands and mountains along the southern border region. ♦ Nearby countries include Belarus, Finland, Kazakhstan, and China. ♦ The climate rages from humid continental to subarctic. Winters vary from cool along the southwest seacoast to frigid in the far northeast. Summers vary from warm in the steppes to cool in the northeast. ♦ There are 37,653 kilometers of coastline. ♦ There are permafrost, volcanic activity, and earthquakes.
Health	♦ The life expectancy is 67 years.

1. What country does this information describe? What information led you to this conclusion?

2.   Give some examples of natural resources found in this country.

3.   Do you think that goods and services in this country are produced using many or few capital resources? What information led you to this conclusion?

4.   Do you think that the human resources in this country possess high levels of human capital? Why?

5.   What is Gross Domestic Product?

6.   The per capita GDP is $7,700. Given this per capita GDP do you think that there are more or fewer goods and services available per person in this country than there are in China? Kenya? Given the per capita GDP of $7,700, how could you determine the GDP of this country?

7.   Do you think that the standard of living in this country is higher or lower than the standard of living in China? Why?

Mystery Country #1   **Kenya**

Mystery Country #2   **China**

Mystery Country #3   **United States**

Mystery Country #4   **France**

Mystery Country #5   **Mexico**

Mystery Country #6   **Egypt**

Mystery Country #7   **Australia**

Mystery Country #8   **Democratic Republic of the Congo**

Mystery Country #9   **Peru**

Mystery Country #10   **Saudi Arabia**

Mystery Country #11   **Czech Republic**

Mystery Country #12   **Ukraine**

LESSON DESCRIPTION

Students participate in a simulation to learn how trade benefits them as individuals and how trade benefits people in different regions and countries. Working in pairs, students learn about the major import and export partners for twelve countries. They identify exports and imports for each country. Using this information, students draw a generalization about how trade benefits consumers.

This trading activity is based on a lesson from *Focus: International Economics*, National Council on Economic Education, 1998.

ECONOMIC CONCEPTS

Exchange (trade)
Imports
Exports

OBJECTIVES – Students will:

- Define exchange, imports, and exports.
- Explain that people voluntarily exchange goods and services because they expect to better off after the exchange.
- Explain that voluntary exchange among people or organizations in different countries gives people a broader range of choices in buying goods and services.
- Explain why countries may import the same type of products that they export.

TIME REQUIRED

Two class periods

MATERIALS

- Paper lunch bag for each student (Evenly number the bags 1 through 5.)
- Small items for trade – variety of candy, variety of stickers, variety of pencils, variety of other items (Place a trade item in each bag.)
- Three small pieces of scrap paper for each student
- Copy of Activity 6.1 cut apart to provide one card per pair of students
- Copy of Activity 6.2 for each pair of students

PROCEDURE
Day One

1.   Ask for examples of exchanges students have made in the last few days. (*money for lunch, an apple from their lunch for a banana from someone else's lunch, money for a haircut*)

2. Generalize that **exchange** takes place when people trade goods and services for other goods and services or for money.

3. Explain that students will participate in an exchange activity. Distribute a paper bag to each student.

4. Tell students to look in the bag but not to tell anyone what is in it. Distribute a piece of scrap paper to each student. Tell students, using a scale of 1 to 5, to decide how satisfied or happy they are with the item in their bags. If they are very happy or satisfied, they should write "5." If they aren't happy at all, they should write "1." A number between 1 and 5 indicates some relative level of happiness.

5. Collect the pieces of scrap paper and add the numbers. On the board, write the heading "Round 1." Under the heading, write the total level of happiness in the classroom.

6. Tell students that each bag has a number 1, 2, 3, 4, or 5 written on it. Tell students to form groups based on the number written on their bags. All students with the number 1 on their bags should be in one group and so on.

7. When students are in their groups, explain that they may now show one another what is in their bags and trade if they want. Trade is not required.

8. Allow a few minutes for students to trade. Distribute a piece of scrap paper to each student. Tell them to rank their level of happiness, using the same scale as before.

9. Collect the pieces of scrap paper and add the numbers. Write the heading "Round 2" on the board. Under the heading, write the total level of happiness in the classroom.

10. Tell students that now they may trade with anyone in the classroom.

11. Allow time for students to trade. Distribute pieces of scrap paper to the students. Have them rate their level of happiness, using the same scale as before.

12. Collect the pieces of scrap paper and add the numbers. Write the heading "Round 3" on the board. Under the heading, write total level of happiness in the classroom. Discuss the following.

    a. What happened to the level of happiness from round one to round two? (*increased*) From round two to round three? (*increased*)

b. Why do you think this happened? (*People were able to trade for an item that they wanted more than the item they had.*)

c. Were you required to make a trade? (*No, trade/exchange was voluntary.*)

d. In which round of this activity was there a greater variety of goods available for consumers? (*the third round*) Why? (*Students could trade with many people who had different goods*)

e. Many people had candy (stickers or pencils); yet, they traded for candy (stickers or pencils). Why? [*wanted a different type of candy (sticker or pencil) than they had, liked the other candy (sticker or pencil) more than the candy (sticker or pencil) they had, wanted some of each type*]

13. Explain that people engage in voluntary exchange because they expect to be better off after the exchange. In this example, students exchanged one item for another because they thought they would be better off (or happier) with the new item than they were with the item they had.

14. Ask why students are willing to exchange $15 for a new T-shirt or for a new CD at a store? [*They want (value) the T-shirt or CD more than they want (value) another good or service that could have been purchased with $15. They expect to be better off with the T-shirt or CD than they will be with anything else they could buy with $15.*]

15. Point out that, similar to the classroom exchange activity, people and organizations in different countries engage in exchange or trade. When people and organizations in different countries export and import goods and services, they are engaged in trade/exchange. **Imports** are foreign goods and services purchased from sellers in other nations. **Exports** are domestic goods and services sold to buyers in other nations.

16. Explain that, similar to the class trading activity, people and organizations from different countries are willing to engage in voluntary exchange because they value the things that they import more than they value the things that they export. They expect to be better off because of the exchange.

17. Point out that trade among people or organizations in different countries also gives them a broader range of choices in buying goods and services. In other words, trade with other countries gives people a larger variety of goods and services to buy. For example, bananas and pineapples are available in the U.S. throughout the year because people in the United States engage in trade with people in Mexico and Costa Rica.

Day Two

1. Divide the class into pairs. Give a card from Activity 6.1 and a copy of Activity 6.2 to each pair. Point out the following.

    ♦ Each card lists information about the exports and imports of one of twelve countries. The products listed are the major or largest exports and imports for each country. For example, a major export of Kenya is tea. A major import of Kenya is machinery and transportation equipment.
    ♦ Each table lists major export and import partners for each country. Export partners are those to whom people and organizations in a country sell goods and services they produce. Import partners are those from whom people and organizations in a country buy goods and services.

2. Explain that to make discussion easier, students will list information about each country on Activity 6.2. Tell students to write the name of the country in the circle on the chart.

3. Explain that one member of the pair is to read the information from the card to the other member who should record the information in the appropriate box on the chart. For example, one member of the pair will read the list of exports while the other records the goods and services in the box labeled "Exports" on Activity 6.2. Tell students to list the names of countries in the "Trading Partners" box to whom their country exports goods and services and from whom their country imports goods and services.

4. After students have completed the work, each pair will be asked to share import and export information about its country with the rest of the class.

5. When students have completed the work, allow time for them to share information with the class. Tell students that they should listen for information to answer the questions on the handout.

6. When the presentations are complete, discuss the following.

    a. Most often, are major trading partners nearby or far from one another? (*nearby*) Why? (*The less distance between the countries, the easier and less expensive it is to trade.*)
    b. Why don't the people in a country produce all goods and services they want? (*They do not have all the necessary resources to produce all products they want.*)
    c. The largest import and export trading partners for the United States are Canada, Mexico, and Japan. How are these three countries similar? (*Canada and Mexico are located*

near the United States. Canada, Japan and the United States are industrial countries.)

  d. Who is Mexico's largest import partner? (*United States*)
     Who is Mexico's largest export partner? (*United States*)

7. Point out that many of the countries the students learned about imported the same type of goods that they exported. This happens frequently with other countries as well. For example, people in Japan export cars to people in the United States and Germany. However, people in Japan also import cars from the United States and Germany.

8. Remind students that in the trading activity some traded candy for candy, pencils for pencils, or stickers for stickers. Candy is a broad category of production. There are many different kinds of candy. Specialization occurs within candy production. There are candy manufacturers who specialize only in chocolate candy. People specialize in the production of one type of candy and trade for another type.

9. Explain that similar things happen with trade between people and organizations in different countries. For example, another production category is commercial aircraft. The aircraft industry in the USA exports large commercial airliners. However, American airlines import small commercial planes and large commercial aircraft that differ from those produced in the United States.

10. Have students look at their import and export information about the twelve countries to find other examples of countries importing products similar to products they export. (*Kenya exports petroleum products and imports petroleum products – it may be that they export kerosene and import gasoline. Egypt exports chemicals and imports chemicals – it is likely that they export one type of chemical(s) and import others. Australia imports machinery and transport equipment and exports machinery and transport equipment, but probably it imports different machinery and transport equipment. Czech Republic exports the same list of products it imports – again it is likely that they are importing different raw materials and fuels than they export and so on.*)

11. Emphasize that people and organizations in different countries often import the same type of products they export because the product produced in one country differs in some way from the product produced in the other country. The differences make the products desirable in the other country. For example, Japanese cars imported to the U. S. are in some way different from U. S. cars. These differences make the cars desirable to those in the United States.

12. Have students post their copies of Activity 6.2 on a wall or bulletin board and create a title for the board, "Charting Imports and Exports." (See extension activities 1 and 2 for additions to the bulletin board display.)

CLOSURE

Review the key points of the lesson using the following discussion questions.

1. What is exchange? (*people trading goods and services for other goods and services or for money*)

2. Why do people participate in voluntary exchange? (*They expect to be better off.*)

3. Give examples of times you engaged in voluntary exchange. (*using money to buy food, movie tickets, and other goods and services; trading lunch items at school*)

4. Why are you willing to exchange money for food, a movie ticket or other goods and services? (*value the food or movie ticket more than other things that could be purchased with the money; expect to be better off*)

5. Why are you willing to exchange an item from your lunch for an item from someone else's lunch? (*value it more than the item they have; expect to be better off*)

6. What are imports? (*foreign goods and services purchased from sellers in other nations*)

7. Give examples of products the United States imports. (*shoes, clothing, cars, machinery*)

8. What are exports? (*domestic goods and services sold to buyers in other nations*)

9. Give examples of products the United States exports. (*cars, machinery, computers, software, movies, agricultural products*)

10. When you were able to trade with more students in the classroom, what happened to the number and type of goods available? (*There were more and different types of goods available.*)

11. When people in one country trade with people in other countries, what happens to the amount and type of goods available? (*There are more goods available. There's a larger variety of goods available.*)

12. Why do countries export products similar to products they import? (*Because specialization occurs within broader production categories, one country produces a product that in some way differs from the product produced in another country.*)

13. From the countries studied, give an example of a product a country imports that is similar to a product that same country exports. (*U.S. – airplanes, cars; Czech Republic – raw materials; Egypt – chemicals; Australia – machinery*)

ASSESSMENT

Have students answer the following questions.

1. Why do people and organizations in the United States import the same type of products that they export, such as cars and airplanes?

2. If people in your state were only able to trade with other people in the state, what would happen to the variety of goods and services available in your state?

3. Serena gave Mike the yogurt from her lunch in exchange for his apple. Why were Serena and Mike willing to make this exchange?

EXTENSION

1. Have students check at home for items from the twelve countries in Activity 6.1. Create a list of the number and types of products imported from these countries. Have students answer the following questions.

   ♦ Are these products similar to products produced in the United States?
   ♦ Why did your family purchase these products?

2. Have students create a graph representing the quantities of imports the class identified from each country. Have students add these charts and other information they acquired to the bulletin board display created at the end of the lesson.

Country	Kenya
Exports	tea, coffee, horticultural products, petroleum products, fish, cement
Export Value	$1.8 billion (2001 est.)
Export Partners	United Kingdom, Tanzania, Uganda, Germany
Imports	machinery and transportation equipment, petroleum products, iron and steel, resins and plastics
Import Value	$3.1 billion (2001 est.)
Import Partners	United Kingdom, United Arab Emirates, Japan, India

Country	China
Exports	machinery and equipment, textiles and clothing, footwear, toys and sporting goods, mineral fuels
Export Value	$262.1 billion (2001 est.)
Export Partners	United States, Hong Kong, Japan, South Korea, Germany, Netherlands, United Kingdom, Singapore, Taiwan
Imports	machinery and equipment, mineral fuels, plastics, iron and steel, chemicals
Import Value	$236.2 billion (2001 est.)
Import Partners	Japan, Taiwan, United States, South Korea, Germany, Hong Kong, Russia, Malaysia

Country	United States
Exports	capital goods, automobiles, industrial supplies and raw materials, consumer goods, agricultural products
Export Value	$723 billion (2001 est.)
Export Partners	Canada, Mexico, Japan, United Kingdom, Germany, France, Netherlands
Imports	crude oil and refined petroleum products, machinery, automobiles, consumer goods, industrial raw materials, food, and beverages
Import Value	$1.148 trillion (2001 est.)
Import Partners	Canada, Japan, Mexico, China, Germany, United Kingdom, Taiwan

Sources: *The World Factbook 2002*, http://www.cia.gov/cia/publications/factbook/index.html, Central Intelligence Agency; and *The Statesman's Yearbook 2001*, St. Martin's Press, New York, NY.

Country	France
Exports	machinery and transportation equipment, aircraft, plastics, chemicals, pharmaceutical products, iron and steel, beverages
Export Value	$293.3 billion (2001 est.)
Export Partners	European Union (especially Germany, United Kingdom, Spain, Italy, Belgium-Luxembourg), United States
Imports	machinery and equipment, vehicles, crude oil, aircraft, plastics, chemicals
Import Value	$292.6 billion (2001)
Import Partners	European Union (especially Germany, Belgium-Luxembourg, Italy, United Kingdom) and United States (2000 est.)

Country	Mexico
Exports	manufactured goods, oil and oil products, silver, fruits, vegetables, coffee, and cotton
Export Value	$159 billion (2001)
Export Partners	United States, Canada, Germany, Spain, Netherlands Antilles, Japan, United Kingdom, Venezuela
Imports	metal-working machines, steel mill products, agricultural machinery, electrical equipment, car parts for assembly, repair parts for motor vehicles, aircraft, and aircraft parts
Import Value	$168 billion (2001)
Import Partners	United States, Japan, Germany, Canada, China, South Korea, Taiwan, Italy, Brazil

Country	Egypt
Exports	crude oil and petroleum products, cotton, textiles, metal products, chemicals
Export Value	$7.1 billion (2001 est.)
Export Partners	EU (Italy, Germany, United Kingdom), United States, Middle East, Asian countries
Imports	machinery and equipment, foodstuffs, chemicals, wood products, fuels
Import Value	$16.4 billion (2001 est.)
Import Partners	EU (Germany, Italy, France), United States, Asian countries, Middle East

Sources: *The World Factbook 2001*, http://www.cia.gov/cia/publications/factbook/index.html, Central Intelligence Agency; and *The Statesman's Yearbook 2001*, St. Martin's Press, New York, NY.

Country	Australia
Exports	coal, gold, meat, wool, alumina, iron ore, wheat, machinery and transport equipment
Export Value	$68.8 billion (2001 est.)
Export Partners	Japan, United States, South Korea, China, New Zealand, Singapore
Imports	machinery and transport equipment, computers and office machines, telecommunication equipment and parts, crude oil and petroleum products
Import Value	$70.2 billion (2001 est.)
Import Partners	Unites States, Japan, China, United Kingdom, Germany, South Korea, New Zealand, Malaysia

Country	Democratic Republic of the Congo
Exports	diamonds, copper, coffee, cobalt, crude oil
Export Value	$750 million (2001 est.)
Export Partners	Benelux (Belgium, Netherlands, Luxembourg), United States, South Africa, Finland, Italy
Imports	foodstuffs, mining and other machinery, transport equipment, fuels
Import Value	$1.024 billion (2001 est.)
Import Partners	South Africa, Benelux (Belgium, Netherlands, Luxembourg) Nigeria, Kenya, China

Country	Peru
Exports	fish and fish products, gold, copper, zinc, crude petroleum and by products, lead, coffee, sugar, and cotton
Export Value	$7.3 billion (2001 est.)
Export Partners	United States, United Kingdom, Switzerland, China, Japan, Chile, Brazil
Imports	machinery, transport equipment, foodstuffs, petroleum, iron and steel, chemicals, pharmaceuticals
Import Value	$7.3 billion (2001 est.)
Import Partners	United States, Chile, Spain, Venezuela, Colombia, Brazil, Japan

Sources: *The World Factbook 2002*, http://www.cia.gov/cia/publications/factbook/index.html, Central Intelligence Agency; and *The Statesman's Yearbook 2001*, St. Martin's Press, New York, NY.

Country	Saudi Arabia
Exports	petroleum and petroleum products
Export Value	$66.9 billion (2001)
Export Partners	United States, Japan, South Korea, Singapore, India
Imports	machinery and equipment, foodstuffs, chemicals, motor vehicles, textiles
Import Value	$29.7 billion (2001)
Import Partners	United States, Japan, Germany, United Kingdom

Country	Czech Republic
Exports	machinery and transport equipment, other manufactured goods, chemicals, raw materials and fuel
Export Value	$32.7 billion (2000)
Export Partners	Germany, Slovakia, Austria, Poland, United Kingdom
Imports	machinery and transport equipment, other manufactured goods, chemicals, raw materials, fuels
Import Value	$37.4 billion (2000)
Import Partners	Germany, Russia, Slovakia, Italy, Austria

Country	Ukraine
Exports	ferrous and nonferrous metals, fuel and petroleum products, machinery and transport equipment, food products
Export Value	$17.3 billion (2001 est.)
Export Partners	Russia, Turkey, Italy, Germany
Imports	energy, machinery and parts, transportation equipment, chemicals
Import Value	$17.1 billion (2001 est.)
Import Partners	Russia, Turkmenistan, Germany, United States

Sources: *The World Factbook 2002*, http://www.cia.gov/cia/publications/factbook/index.html, Central Intelligence Agency; and *The Statesman's Yearbook 2001*, St. Martin's Press, New York, NY.

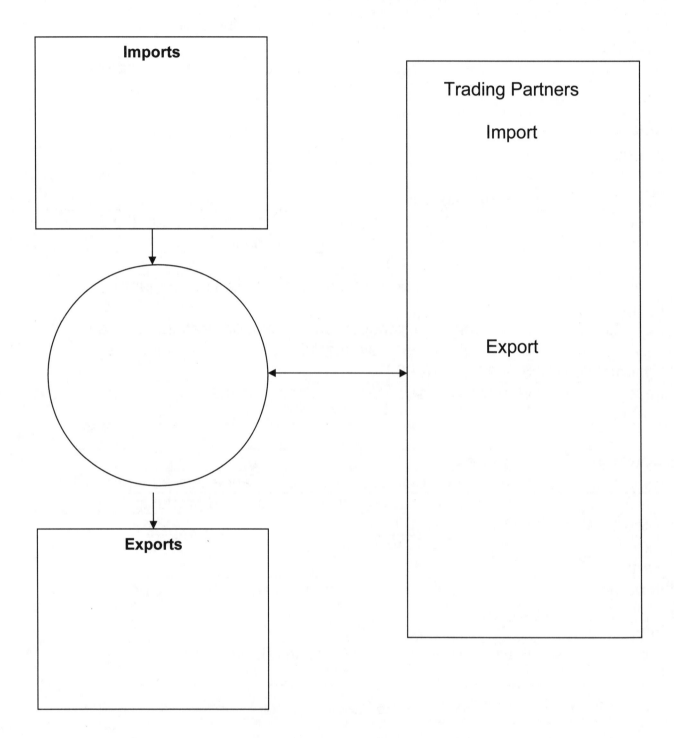

LESSON DESCRIPTION

Using numerical examples and bar graphs, students see why it benefits two countries to specialize in the production of one of two products and then trade with each other, even if one country has the resources and technology to produce more of either good than the other country. The last section of this lesson can be used as a challenge activity.

Students must be able to make and read bar graphs in order to complete this lesson.

ECONOMIC CONCEPTS

Exchange (trade)
Specialization
Opportunity cost
Comparative advantage

OBJECTIVES – Students will:

- Define specialization, division of labor, and exchange (trade).
- Explain that production and consumption are increased when nations specialize and trade.
- Define opportunity cost and comparative advantage.
- Explain that comparative advantage is the basis for the gains from trade for both individual workers and for people and businesses engaged in international trade.

TIME REQUIRED

Three to four class periods

MATERIALS

- One copy of Activities 7.1, 7.2, 7.3, and 7.4 for each student
- Red and blue colored pencil for each student
- Red and blue transparency pens
- Transparency of "Beta" page of Activity 7.2
- Transparency of Activity 7.3

PROCEDURE

1. To pique student interest, discuss the following.

    a. Is it a good idea for people and businesses in the United States to trade with people and businesses in other countries, or would it be better for people in the United States to try to make everything themselves? Why? (*Answers will vary*.)
    b. Give examples of products that cannot be produced in the United States or that cannot be produced at levels high enough to satisfy the current demand. (*diamonds and oil*)

c. Do people and businesses in different states in the United States trade with one another? (*Yes.*) Give examples of products people and businesses in your state buy from or sell to people and businesses in other states. (*Answers will vary.*)

2. Point out that people seem to accept the idea that specialization and trade among individuals living in the same country is a good thing. In fact, this has been going on for thousands of years. Discuss the following.

   a. Give examples of surnames that are also the names of occupations. (*Carpenter, Painter, Butcher, and Smith*). Note: If some students speak a language other than English, have them suggest examples in those languages.
   b. How do you think people came to have these last names? (*These were the jobs the people did.*)

3. Explain that people specialized in particular jobs. As a result, they came to be known by the name of their occupation. Ask why people don't make all the goods and services they consume for themselves. (*It isn't efficient; it is time consuming; some simply wouldn't be able to do it.*)

4. Explain that in historical and fictional settings where people had to be self-sufficient, or close to it, people lived very hard lives with very few goods and services. "Mountain men" fur trappers, and later the early settlers who lived miles from anyone else with only horses, wagons, or walking as a means of transportation are good examples. The fictional Robinson Crusoe and Swiss Family Robinson had to be self-sufficient.

5. Explain that **specialization** occurs when people, regions, or nations produce a narrower range of goods and services than they consume. For example, a pediatrician produces medical care for children but consumes clothing, food, shelter entertainment, and adult medical care produced by others.

6. Explain that **division of labor** means breaking down a production process into several different steps, usually with different people or even workers in different occupations performing different parts of the production process. Discuss the following.

   a. Give examples of specialization in our school and community. (*gym teacher, reading specialist, mathematics teachers, pediatricians, family practitioners, mechanics, accountants, truck drivers, bus drivers*)

b. What products have you produced at school or at home
    using division of labor? (*Answers will vary but might include
    meals at home and group projects at school.*)

c. What are some benefits of specialization and the division of
    labor? (*More goods or services can usually be produced in
    the same amount of time.*)

d. Why do you think people are able to produce more goods
    and services when they specialize and use division of labor?
    (*People learn by doing, or, as the saying goes, "Practice
    makes perfect."*)

7. Explain that another important reason for the increased
    production is that as production becomes more specialized, new
    tools and machines are often developed to use in these
    specialized jobs. With specialized tools and machines, people
    are able to increase production even more.

8. Ask what some costs of specialization and the division of labor
    might be. (*It can be very boring to do one small part of a job
    over and over, day after day, or even year after year. Also, if
    you only make one thing or just a few things, you must depend
    on others to make the rest of the goods and services you
    consume or use in your job.*)

9. Given that people within communities, states, and countries
    benefit from specialization and trade, does the same thing hold
    true with international trade between people in two or more
    countries? If so, why? Explain that in this lesson students will
    investigate these questions. Distribute a copy of Activity 7.1 to
    each student, and allow time for the students to read the activity.

10. When students have finished reading, distribute a copy of
    Activity 7.2 and a red and blue colored pencil to each student.
    Display a transparency of Activity 7.2. Explain that students will
    produce bar graphs to represent each of the five mana/dud
    production combinations for Beta and for Zoid.

11. Using red and blue transparency pens, demonstrate how to
    complete the graph for Beta's combinations A and B as follows.

    ◆ Beta combination "A" is 0 duds and 400 mana. There will be
       no bar for duds.
    ◆ Leave the first half of the "A" column empty.
    ◆ Create a bar by coloring rows 100 through 400 with the red
       marker in the other half of this column.
    ◆ Beta combination "B" is 400 duds and 300 mana.
    ◆ Create a bar that requires half the column by coloring rows
       100 through 400 blue. This represents the production of
       duds in combination "B."

♦ Create a second bar that requires the second half of the column by coloring rows 100 through 300 red. This represents the production of mana in combination "B."

12. Tell students to complete the rest of the Beta graph and the entire Zoid graph. When students have finished, tell them to place the graphs next to one another. Point out that each country had to choose to produce only one of the five combinations of mana and duds.

13. Explain that these tables are based on 100 workers, so the total production levels in the countries would depend on how many hundreds of workers were working in each country. Discuss the following.

   a. If the people of Beta decided to produce combination B instead of combination A, what changes would occur? (*They would have 100 fewer mana to consume and 400 additional duds to consume.*)

   b. If the people of Zoid decided to produce combination C instead of combination D, what changes would occur? (*They would have 100 fewer duds to consume and 50 more mana to consume.*)

14. Tell the students that initially, the people in Beta chose combination D and the people in Zoid chose combination D. Explain that people in both countries wanted to have more mana and more duds to consume, but there were a lot of other things they wanted to produce and consume, too. They decided not to increase the total number of workers producing mana and duds, or the amount of land and other resources used to produce these two products.

15. Distribute a copy of Activity 7.3 to each student and display a transparency of Activity 7.3. Tell students to read the paragraph at the top of the page. Tell students to refer to the bar graphs from Activity 7.2 and discuss the following.

   a. Beta and Zoid both chose combination D, enter the mana and dud production for both countries in the table. What would the total "Beta and Zoid World" production of mana be? (*150 units*) Enter this amount in the table on the transparency and have students enter the information in their tables.

   b. How many mana would be available for people to consume in the "Beta and Zoid World?" (*150 units*)

   c. If Beta and Zoid both chose combination D, what would the total "Beta and Zoid World" production of duds be? (*1500 units*) Enter this amount in the table on the transparency and have students enter the information in their tables.

d. How many duds would be available for people to consume in the "Beta and Zoid World?" (*1500 units*)

e. According to the visiting economist, there's a way the countries could get more mana and more duds without using any more resources. Can you see how the people in Beta and Zoid can both get more mana and duds to consume? (*Answers will vary*.)

f. If the people of Beta used all their resources to produce duds, how many duds would be produced? (*1600 units*) How much mana would be produced in Beta? (*0 units*) Enter this amount in the second table on the transparency. Tell students to enter this amount in their tables.

g. If the people of Zoid used all their resources to produce mana, how much mana would be produced? (*200 units*) How many duds would be produced in Zoid? (*0 units*) Enter this amount in the second table on the transparency and tell students to enter it in their tables.

h. How much mana is available for consumption in the Beta and Zoid world now? (*200 units*) How many duds are available for consumption in the Beta and Zoid world now? (*1600 units*)

16. Point out that the world production of duds and mana increases if the two countries specialize. However, all duds are in Beta and all mana is in Zoid. This means that the people in the two countries must trade. All people in Beta and Zoid will have MORE duds and mana to consume if they specialize and trade. This is what the economist meant!

17. Point out that students looked at bar graphs and found that people in both Beta and Zoid would be better off (could consume more mana and more duds) if they specialized. Economists also make this determination buy looking at the real cost of producing these goods in each country.

18. Explain that to determine the real cost, students must figure out how many mana people in each country give up when one worker moves from producing mana to producing duds. They must also determine how many duds people in each country must give up when one worker moves from producing duds to producing mana.

19. Distribute a copy of Activity 7.4 to each student. Tell students they may work with a partner or in a small group. Have students read the handout and answer the questions. When students have finished working, discuss the following.

a. In Beta, when one more worker starts producing duds, by how much does the production of duds increase? (*16 units*) How much does the production of mana decrease? (*4 units*)

b. How many units of mana do the people of Beta give up to get one more unit of duds? (*¼ unit of mana; 16/4=1/x; x = ¼ unit*)

c. What is the real cost of 1 unit of duds in Beta? (*¼ unit of mana*)

d. In Beta, when one more worker starts producing mana, by how much does the production of mana increase? (*4 units*) How much does the production of duds decrease? (*16 units*)

e. How many units of duds do the people of Beta give up to get one more unit of mana? (*4 units of duds; 4/16 = 1/x; x = 4*)

f. What is the real cost of 1 unit of mana in Beta? (*4 units of duds*)

g. In Zoid, when one more worker starts producing duds, by how much does the production of duds increase? (*4 units*) How much does the production of mana decrease? (*2 units*)

h. How many units of mana do the people of Zoid give up to get one more unit of duds? (*½ unit; 4/2 = 1/x; x = ½ unit*)

i. What is the real cost of one unit of duds? (*½ unit of mana*)

j. In Zoid, when one more worker starts producing mana, by how much does the production of mana increase? (*2 units*) How much does the production of duds decrease? (*4 units*)

k. How many units of duds do the people of Zoid give up to get one more unit of mana? (*2 units; 2/4 = 1/x; x = 2 units*)

l. What is the real cost of one unit of mana? (*2 units of duds*)

20. Explain that when goods and services are produced in the country where the real cost of production is lower, resources are being used more efficiently so more goods and services can be produced. As a result, more goods and services are available for consumption. Discuss the following.

a. Which country has the lower real cost of producing mana? (*Zoid*) How do you know this? (*Zoid gives up 2 duds for every unit of mana it produces. Beta gives up 4 duds for every unit of mana it produces.*)

b. Which country has the lower real cost of producing duds? (*Beta*) How do you know this? (*Beta gives up ¼ unit of mana for every dud it produces. Zoid gives up ½ unit of mana for every dud it produces.*)

21. Explain that the real cost of something is also called the opportunity cost. **Opportunity cost** is the highest-valued alternative that is given up when a choice is made. When the people of Beta or Zoid decide to produce another unit of mana, the opportunity cost is the amount of duds they give up. When they decide to produce another unit of duds, the opportunity cost is the mana they give up.

22. Explain that a famous economist, David Ricardo, developed the theory of comparative advantage. **Comparative advantage**

means that people specialize in the production of a good or
service for which they have a lower opportunity cost and trade
for other goods and services.

23.   Ask which country had the comparative advantage in the
      production of duds? (*Beta*) the production of Mana? (*Zoid*)

24.   Point out that determining in which product the people of Beta
      and Zoid have comparative advantage, also demonstrates that
      the people in both countries will be better off if they specialize—
      there will be more duds and mana produced and available for
      consumption. Specialization and trade according to comparative
      advantage make it possible for people to have more from their
      limited resources.

Optional Challenge Activity

1.   Explain that through specialization the total production of mana
      and duds has gone up, but now all mana is produced in Zoid,
      and all duds in Beta. To take advantage of the increased
      production levels, the countries must trade with each other.
      Trade (exchange) is exchanging goods and services with people
      for other goods and services or for money.

2.   Ask at what price people in the two countries will trade mana
      and duds. Remind students that in Beta, the real cost of
      producing mana is 4 units of duds, so as long as the people of
      Beta can buy mana for less than 4 duds, they will be better off.

3.   Remind students that in Zoid, the real cost of mana is 2 units of
      duds, so as long as the people of Zoid can sell mana for more
      than 2 units of duds they will be better off.

4.   Explain that this means if people in the countries trade an
      amount between 2 and 4 units of mana for every unit of duds,
      people in both countries will gain from trade.

5.   Explain that this range of trade can also be determined by
      looking at the real costs of duds. In Zoid, the real cost of
      producing a unit of duds is ½ unit of mana. As long as the
      people of Zoid can buy duds for less than ½ unit of mana, they
      will be better off. In Beta, the real cost of producing a unit of
      duds is ¼ unit of mana, so as long as the people of Beta can sell
      duds for more than ¼ unit of mana they will be better off.

6.   Read the following scenario.

      *Suppose that Beta and Zoid specialize in production and agree
      to trade mana and duds at the "price" of 3 units of duds for each
      unit of mana and Zoid agrees to sell Beta 125 units of mana.*

7. Discuss the following.

   a. How many units of mana and duds will Beta have? (*Beta will produce 1600 units of duds, but trade 375 units to Zoid in exchange for 125 units of mana. That leaves Beta with 1,225 units of duds and 125 units of mana.*)

   b. How many units of mana and duds will Zoid have? (*Zoid will produce 200 units of mana, but trade 125 units to Beta in exchange for 375 units of duds. That leaves Zoid with 75 units of mana and 375 units of duds.*) Note: This is the midpoint of the trading range that makes both countries better off. The two countries might not end up exactly at that midpoint. Depending on the relative bargaining power of the two countries, it might be closer to either 2 or 4 units of duds per unit of mana. It won't be more or less than that, however, because then there would be no incentive for both countries to trade.

   c. Which country gained from this trade, compared to its position before the two countries specialized and traded? (*Both countries gained. Compared to its original, non-trading level of 100 mana and 1200 duds, Beta ends up with 25 more units of both mana and duds. Compared to its original level of 50 mana and 300 duds, Zoid gains 25 units of mana and 75 units of duds.*) There were 100 workers involved in production in each country. How much more, on average, would be available for each of these workers to consume? (*For each day of production, each worker in Beta gains, on average, ¼ units of both mana and duds. In Zoid, the average gain for each worker is ¼ unit of mana and ¾ units of duds.*)

8. Explain that when the average level of goods and services available for people to consume increases, material standards of living rise; that is, people have more goods and services on average.

9. Remind students that comparative advantage is the ability to produce a good or service at a lower opportunity cost (also called real cost). Beta had the comparative advantage in producing duds and Zoid had the comparative advantage in producing mana.

10. Explain that comparative advantage determines which goods or services a person or people in a country should specialize in producing. Other people and countries will have a comparative advantage in producing other goods and services, which establishes the mutual gains for trading.

11. Display the transparency of Visual 7.3. Point out how the specialization in Beta and Zoid led to an increase in the production of both mana and duds. That means consumption of both products can increase, too. More generally, explain that as production and consumption of food, clothing, and other goods and services increase, material standards of living are improving.

12. Explain that even large, industrialized nations that could potentially produce more of almost any product than smaller, less industrialized nations will benefit by specializing and trading. This happens because, in all nations, resources can potentially be used to produce many different things, but once the choice is made to use them to produce one product, they can't be used to produce something else. Differences in these real or opportunity costs establish the potential gains from specialization and trade among all different kinds of nations, and also between nations that have similar kinds of economies and labor forces, just as they do for specialization and trade by individual workers who live in the same country.

13. Because of the gains from specialization and trade, it doesn't make sense for either individual workers or countries to try to produce all the goods and services that they consume. There are, however, some problems associated with specialization and trade, including a narrower range of work/jobs (especially in small countries that have to specialize in the production of just a few different products), and greater interdependence with other workers and nations.

CLOSURE

1. Review the key points of the lesson using the following discussion questions.

     a. What is specialization? (*people, as individuals or as regions or nations, producing a narrower range of goods and services than they consume*)
     b. Give examples of specialization in your community or state. (*Answers will vary.*)
     c. What is division of labor? (*breaking a production process down into several different steps*)
     d. Give an example of a time that you used division of labor to produce something at home or at school. (*lemonade stand with friends, making dinner—dad cooks, child sets table, mom cleans up, group project/work for school*)
     e. What is a benefit of specialization and division of labor? (*More goods and services are produced with the same amount of resources.*)
     f. Why are people able to produce more goods and services when they specialize and use division of labor? (*They get*

better/faster because they do the same thing over and over;
they develop special tools to help them produce.)

g. What are some costs of specialization? (*boring, makes*
people dependent on one another)

h. What is comparative advantage? (*People specialize in the*
production of a good or service for which they have a lower
opportunity cost and trade for other goods and services.)

i. What is the benefit to specialization and trade according to
comparative advantage? (*They make it possible for people*
to have more from their limited resources.)

2. Remind students that just as with specialization by workers in
the same country, international specialization and trade allows
production levels to increase, which means that consumption
levels increase and material standards of living are also
increased. The average number of duds and mana available for
workers in Beta and Zoid to consume as a result of
specialization and trade increased—their standard of living
improved.

3. Remind students that the basis for specialization and trade, both
for individual workers and nations, is comparative advantage.
Discuss the following.

a. What is trade? (*exchange of goods and services with*
people for other goods and services or for money)

b. What is comparative advantage? [*producing the good or*
service for which you have the lower real cost (opportunity
cost)]

c. What is opportunity cost? (*the highest-valued alternative*
that is given up when a choice is made)

4. Remind students that this lesson began by having them identify
work in which some individual workers specialized. What are
some products that particular countries specialize in – selling
these products not only to people and organizations in that
country, but in other countries as well? (*United States –*
automobiles, computer software, large commercial jets, and
agricultural products; Canada – timber products, automobiles,
small commercial jets, and agricultural products; Western Europe
– steel, wines, clothing and automobiles; Japan – electronics
automobiles, and cameras; Latin America – clothing and textiles,
small airplanes, agricultural products)

5. Point out that specialization in these countries takes place even to
the degree that some sell (export) some types of a product, but
buy (import) other types of the same product. For example, the
United States exports pickup trucks and SUVs, but imports many
smaller automobiles, and several brands and models of luxury and
sports cars.

ASSESSMENT

Have students write an essay comparing the skills and training required to enter a particular occupation (for example, doctor, dentist, professional athlete, carpenter, salesperson, or construction worker) and the kinds of resources (including human resources, capital goods, and natural resources) that have made it possible for some countries to specialize in the production of particular kinds of goods and services, which they sell (export) to other countries. In both cases, have students discuss why some people and countries will be able to produce these goods and services more effectively – at a lower real or opportunity cost – than other people and countries.

EXTENSION

1. Assign students or teams of students two or three countries, and have them prepare a report on the major imports and exports of those countries in recent years. Have the students discuss why the resources (natural, human, and capital) in these countries lead them to specialize in the production of the products they export.

2. Have students or teams of students prepare a report on the major imports and exports of the United States today, 50 years ago, and 100 years ago. This report should discuss how changes in the resource base in this country, and in other countries, changed over this period of time, leading to changes in what was produced domestically and what was imported from other countries.

3. Teach lesson six, "Trading Connections," from *The Wide World of Trade.*

Long ago, in a galaxy far, far away, there was only one planet able to sustain life. On this planet there was only one continent, and on that continent there were only two countries, Beta and Zoid. Beta was a large, prosperous country. Its people were well educated, and its factories and offices employed the newest machines, computers, and other technology. Zoid was a much smaller and poorer country. A large percentage of its people had dropped out of school after seven or eight years to help support their families. There were only a few factories in Zoid, and most of those had old equipment, with few computers available to workers or managers. Workers at many stores and banks still did calculations using an abacus.

Two of the major products that people in both Beta and Zoid liked to consume were mana (food) and duds (clothing). Both countries had to make a basic choice about how to produce these products. Either both countries could try to produce both goods, or the two countries could each specialize in the production of one good and then trade for the other good.

At first, people in both countries decided to produce both products and not to trade with the other country. The people in Beta thought, "What can we gain from trading with such a small, poor country?" And people in Zoid thought, "How can we compete with workers in Beta, who have more education and so many more machines to use to make mana and duds?"

Production data for workers in the two countries were used by some people to support this position. In one day, one worker in Beta could produce either 4 units of mana or 16 units of duds. On Zoid, one worker could produce either 2 units of mana or 4 units of duds.

Both countries had limited resources, so the people in both countries had to decide how much of each product to make. Of course, when a country used more resources to make mana, it couldn't produce as many duds, and when it used more resources to make duds, it couldn't produce as much mana.

The table below shows five possible combinations of mana and duds production Beta has using 100 workers and the other resources used to produce these goods as efficiently as possible, given the available land, factories, and other resources in Beta.

Beta Production Combinations

Products \ Amounts	A	B	C	D	E
Mana	400	300	200	100	0
Duds	0	400	800	1200	1600

Use the data from the table above to create bar graphs illustrating each production combination for Beta. Use a red colored pencil to represent mana and a blue colored pencil to represent duds.

	duds	mana	duds	mana	duds	mana	duds	mana	duds	mana
1600										
1500										
1400										
1300										
1200										
1100										
1000										
900										
800										
700										
600										
500										
400										
300										
200										
100										
	A		B		C		D		E	

The table below shows five possible combinations of mana and duds production Zoid has using 100 workers and the other resources used to produce these goods as efficiently as possible, given the available land, factories, and other resources in Zoid.

Zoid Production Combinations

Products / Amounts	A	B	C	D	E
Mana	200	150	100	50	0
Duds	0	100	200	300	400

Use the data from the table above to create bar graphs illustrating each production combination for Beta. Use a red colored pencil to represent mana and a blue colored pencil to represent duds.

Zoid Production Combinations

	duds	mana	duds	mana	duds	mana	duds	mana	duds	mana
1600										
1500										
1400										
1300										
1200										
1100										
1000										
900										
800										
700										
600										
500										
400										
300										
	A		B		C		D		E	

Things went on this way for some time, until an economist visiting from the planet Ricardo held a press conference to say that she knew how the countries could get more mana and more duds without using any more resources. Can you see how Beta and Zoid can both get more mana and duds to consume?

World Production of Beta and Zoid
If Both Countries Chose Production Combination D

Product	Beta	Zoid	World
Mana			
Duds			

World Production of Beta and Zoid
If Beta Specialized in Duds and Zoid Specialized in Mana

Product	Beta	Zoid	World
Mana			
Duds			

Remember that in one day, one worker in Beta could produce either 4 units of mana or 16 units of duds. In Zoid, one worker could produce either 2 units of mana or 4 units of duds.

Use this information to complete the following statements.

A.   In Beta, when one more worker starts producing duds, the production of duds goes up by _____ units and the production of mana goes down by _____ unit(s).

B.   The people of Beta give up 4 units of mana to get 16 more units of duds. How many units of mana do they give up to get 1 more unit of duds? _____

C.   This means that the real cost of 1 unit of duds in Beta is _____ units of mana.

D.   In Beta, when one more worker starts producing mana, the production of mana goes up by _____ units and the production of duds goes down by _____ units.

E.   The people of Beta give up 16 units of duds to get 4 more units of mana. How many . units of duds do they give up to get one more unit of mana? _____

F.   This means the real cost of 1 unit of mana in Beta is _____ units of duds.

G.   In Zoid, when one more worker starts producing duds, the production of duds goes up by _____ units and the production of mana goes down by _____ units.

H.   The people of Zoid give up 2 units of mana to get 4 more units of duds. How many units of mana do they give up to get 1 more unit of duds? _____

I.   This means that the real cost of 1 unit of duds in Zoid is _____ unit of mana.

J.   In Zoid, when one more worker starts producing mana, the production of mana goes up by _____ units and the production of duds goes down by _____ units.

K.   The people of Zoid give up 4 units of duds to get 2 more units of mana. How many units of duds do they give up to get 1 more unit of mana? _____

L.   This means that the real cost of 1 unit of mana in Zoid is _____ units of duds.

M.   In which country is the real cost of producing one unit of mana lower? _____

N.   In which country is the real cost of producing one unit of duds lower? _____

O.   How can the countries use this information so that both countries get more mana and more duds to consume?

LESSON DESCRIPTION

The class is divided into two groups that participate in a simulation making two types of postcards. In the first round, each group specializes and then considers possible results from trading for the postcard it didn't produce. In the second round, trade restrictions force each group to produce both types of postcards. Students see how free trade increases worldwide material standards of living and the effects of trade barriers. Different types of trade barriers are defined and examples of each type of trade barrier are presented.

ECONOMIC CONCEPTS

Imports
Exports
Trade Barriers
Tariff
Quota
Embargo
Subsidy
Standard
Specialization

OBJECTIVES – Students will:

- Define trade barrier, tariff, quota, embargo, subsidy, and standard.
- Explain why world output increases when countries specialize and trade freely.
- Explain the effects of trade barriers.

TIME REQUIRED

One to two class periods

MATERIALS

- Transparencies of Visuals 8.1, 8.2, and Activity 8.3
- One copy of Activities 8.3, 8.4, and 8.5 for each student
- Country A large resource bag with the following.
    1. Large supply of Activity 8.1
    2. Large supply of plain 8 ½ " x 11" paper
    3. Pencil, one for every two students
    4. Markers, one for every two students
    5. Large supply of paper clips
    6. Scissors, one for every two students
- Country B large resource bag with the following.
    1. Large supply of Activity 8.2
    2. Large supply of plain 8 ½" x 11" paper
    3. Single hole punch, one for every two students
    4. Scissors, one for every two students
    5. Ruler, one for every two students
    6. Ball of yarn
    7. Markers, one for every two students
    8. Sample triangular and rectangular postcards

PROCEDURE

1. Tell the class that students will represent businesses in two countries that produce triangular postcards and rectangular postcards. Hold up an example of each product.

2. Divide the class into two groups. Give one group the resource bag for Country A and give the resource bag for Country B to the other group.

3. Tell each country to lay out the various resources in its bag. Have "citizens" of the country examine the resources.

4. Tell students that both countries have some resources in common – markers, scissors, pencils, and sheets of plain paper. However, Country A has pencils, paper clips, and paper with printed and decorated rectangles. Country B has paper with printed triangles, single-hole punches, rulers, and yarn.

5. Explain that Country A will specialize in the production of rectangular postcards and Country B will specialize in the production of triangular postcards because their resources are best suited to those products.

6. Tell students that **specialization** occurs when people concentrate their production on fewer kinds of goods and services than they consume.

7. Display Visual 8.1, revealing the instructions for Round 1 only, and review the production steps for each country.

8. Allow times for countries to organize their production. Tell them that they have five minutes to produce as many products as possible. Remind students that they must produce products of good quality.

9. After five minutes, stop production. Tell students to count the number of products produced. Check each country's products for quality and discard any that are poorly made.

10. Display Visual 8.2 and record the number of products each country produced.

11. Remind students that each country specialized in the production of one good over another because of available resources. Discuss the following.

   a. What do you think might happen to the quality of each country's products, if it produced for another round? (*It would improve.*) Why? (*Workers improve their skills the more they practice.*)

b. What do you think might happen to the number of products that are produced if each country produced for another round? (*increase*) Why? (*Workers may reorganize the production process. Some workers might switch jobs because of their skills. With practice, workers are usually able to produce more in the same amount of time.*)

c. What might each country do if it wanted both rectangular and triangular postcards? (*trade*)

d. If each trades one quarter of its postcards, how many cards of each type will Country A have? (*Answers will vary.*) Country B? (*Answers will vary.*) Record information on Visual 8.2.

12. Inform students that they will participate in one more production round. However, this time, trade restrictions between the two countries prohibit them from trading. Each country must produce both goods.

13. Display Visual 8.1. Review production procedures for Round 2. Allow students time to organize production. Remind them they must produce some of each good.

14. Tell students they have five minutes to produce both goods. When the time is up, stop production. Tell students to count up the number of each good produced. Record the numbers on Visual 8.2. Discuss the following

a. What happened to worldwide production of triangular cards? (*decreased*) Rectangular cards? (*decreased*) Why? (*Each country had to shift resources into the production of another good in order to produce some of both goods.*)

b. What was the quality of triangular cards produced in Country A and rectangular postcards in Country B? (*These should be of poorer quality because each country had to produce the second type of postcards by folding and then cutting. They did not have the advantage of having pre-drawn lines. Country A had no hole punches. Country B had no paper clips and had to draw a flower on the postcards.*)

c. Why couldn't countries produce the second good so it would be exactly like the one imported? (*lack of resources, possible lack of skills on the part of workers in folding or drawing, poor technology resources for punching holes and securing pairs of postcards*)

d. In the first round, there was free trade. How did individuals in both countries benefit from free trade? (*When each specialized and traded for the cards they didn't produce, more goods of better quality were available for consumers in both countries.*)

e. How did restricting trade (imposing a trade barrier) affect production of goods in each country and worldwide output? (*Each country produced fewer of the products in which it originally specialized. Each country produced some of the product for which it traded in round one. World production of both products decreased.)*

    f. What do you think might happen to the price of goods when trade is restricted? (*increase*) Why? (*There are fewer goods available than before and a lack of competition.*)

15. Explain that individuals and businesses within countries tend to specialize in the production of specific goods and services based on the resources available, skills of their workers, and technology. These products are sold within the country and some amount may be exported to other countries.

16. Explain that **exports** are goods and services produced in one country and sold to buyers in other nations. In the first production round, which good did Country A export? (*rectangular postcards*) Country B? (*triangular postcards*)

17. Explain that when countries lack certain resources or are unable to produce enough of a good or service with their existing resources to meet the demand for the product within their country, they import goods and services. Tell students that **imports** are foreign goods and services purchased from sellers in other nations. In the first production round, which good did Country A import? (*triangular postcards*) Country B? (*rectangular postcards*)

18. Ask how free trade among individuals and organizations in many countries would affect worldwide material standards of living. (*The standards of living would increase. Individual countries would have more goods and services for their people.*)

19. Tell students that even though free trade increases worldwide material standards of living, governments sometimes choose to impose trade barriers. Define **trade barriers** as government policies that restrict or stop the flow of goods and services among countries.

20. Display a transparency of Activity 8.3. Distribute a copy of Activity 8.3 to each student. Review the types of government-imposed trade barriers by reading the information on Activity 9.3.

21. Divide students into small groups. Give a copy of Activity 8.4 to each student. Tell groups to read the examples of trade barriers and then determine which type of trade barrier each represents.

22. Review student answers. (*1 – standards, 2 – tariff, 3 – quota, 4 – standards, 5 – subsidy, 6 – tariff, 7 – embargo, 8 – quota*)

CLOSURE

Review the key points of the lesson using the following discussion
questions.

1. How do individuals and businesses in countries decide which
    products to produce when they specialize? (*They specialize in
    what they are best at producing based on their available
    resources, technology, and the skill and knowledge of their
    workers.*)

2. How does specialization and trade affect worldwide material
    standards of living? (*Standards of living will increase.*) Explain.
    (*When individuals or organizations in a country specialize and
    produce goods for which they have the resources, skills, and
    knowledge, they tend to produce more goods of better quality
    than if they choose not to specialize. Then they are able to
    trade for products they didn't produce.*)

3. What are imports? (*Foreign goods and services purchased from
    sellers in other nations.*)

4. What are exports? (*Domestic goods and services sold to buyers
    in other countries.*)

5. What are trade barriers? (*Government policies that restrict or
    stop the flow of goods and services among countries.*)

6. What is a tariff? (*A tariff is a tax on imports.*)

7. What is a quota? (*A quota is a limit on the amount of a foreign
    good or service that may be legally imported.*)

8. What is an embargo? (*An embargo prohibits all trade with
    people and businesses in a specific country.*)

9. What are subsidies? (*Subsidies are government payments to
    exporters, which help reduce an exporter's cost of production.*)

10. How can standards serve as trade barriers? (*Standards are
    safety, environmental, health, or other technical requirements
    set by a government. It may be difficult for foreign producers to
    meet these requirements.*)

11. How do trade barriers affect worldwide material standards of
    living? (*They cause standards of living to decrease.*) How?
    (*There are fewer goods available for everyone. There's less
    competition, so consumers pay higher prices. Some goods and
    services are of poorer quality.*)

ASSESSMENT

Distribute a copy of Activity 8.5 to each student. Student answers should explain how the trade barrier they selected would help the orange growers achieve their goal of reducing competition from imported oranges.

EXTENSION

1. Have students use the Internet to locate different examples of the types of trade barriers in place today and in the past.

2. Show the video, "The Protective Tariff Issue, 1832," from *Taxes in U.S. History*, Internal Revenue Service, and teach the lessons that accompany the video.

Tariff – A tariff is a tax on imports. For example, in 1996 the US government imposed a 5.1-cent tariff on every wristwatch imported into the US. If 1000 watches were imported, the US government collected $51.

Quota – A quota is a limit on the amount of a foreign good or service that may be legally imported. Some quotas are voluntary and governments impose some. In the 1980s, the Japanese agreed to export only a certain number of cars to the United States. For many years, the US government has imposed a quota on sugar.

Embargo – An embargo prohibits all trade with people and businesses in a specific country. For example, on August 2, 1990, President Bush imposed a trade embargo on Iraq. Iraqi products could not be imported into the U. S. either directly or through third countries. U.S. products could not be exported from the U.S. or reexported from a third country to Iraq.

Subsidies – Subsidies are government payments to exporters. This payment helps reduce an exporter's cost of production. For example, many countries subsidize the production of cold-rolled steel. Businesses in these countries can export their steel at a lower price than steel produced in the United States.

Standards – Standards are safety, environmental, health, or other technical requirements set by a government. Imports must meet these requirements before they are allowed to come into the country. For example, in the 1990s the US banned the import of all French apples because of a concern over Med fly infestations.

For each example below, identify the type of trade barrier described and write the name of that barrier (tariff, quota, embargo, subsidy, standard) in the space provided.

1. United States refuses to import shrimp from Southeast Asian countries because their shrimpers do not use the types of nets used by U.S. shrimpers that protect sea turtles._____

2. The United States taxes all softwood coming into the US from Canada. _____

3. The U.S. president increases the amount of imported peanuts allowed into the country by 100 million pounds per year.

   _____

4. The European Union prohibits the importing of meat products from animals treated with growth-promoting hormones.

   _____

5. The Australian government gives a grant to manufacturers who produce and export automotive leather. _____

6. In 1996 the US taxed imported grapes, ceramic tableware, motorcycles, bicycles with wheels not exceeding 63.5cm in diameter, and sports footwear of which over 50% of the external surface area was leather. _____

7. In 1963, President Kennedy issued sanctions, which prohibited all trade with Cuba. _____

8. The United States limits the amount of wool suits that Macedonia can ship to the U.S. _____

The United States Orange Growers Association is concerned about increased competition from imported oranges that are larger than those grown in the United States. The Association wants to lobby for a trade barrier.

Some members think a tariff or quota would be most beneficial. Others disagree and suggest an embargo or standards. The largest grower of oranges thinks that none of these trade barriers would be necessary if the United States government would provide growers with a subsidy.

The president of the association must send a letter to the membership explaining which trade barrier, tariff, quota, standard, embargo, or subsidy, he thinks would help the growers achieve their goal to reduce competition from imported oranges. He wants your advice.

Which trade barrier would you recommend? Explain how this barrier will help the orange growers achieve their goal.

Round 1

Country A: Production Steps for Rectangular Postcards

1. Cut out two rectangular postcards.
2. Place two postcards together.
3. Secure with a paperclip.
4. Outline the flowers with a marker.

Country B: Production Steps for Triangular Postcards

1. Cut out two triangles.
2. Place two triangles together and punch a hole.
3. Cut a piece of string 12" long.
4. Place the string through the hole and tie in a bow.

Round 2

Country A: Production Steps for Triangular Postcards

1. Fold the paper into quarters and tear apart.
2. Tear each quarter sheet on the diagonal to make a triangle.
3. Place two triangles together.
4. Punch a hole in the triangles with a pencil.
5. Place a paper clip through the hole.

Country B: Production Steps for Rectangular Postcards

1. Fold the plain paper in half lengthwise cut apart.
2. Fold each half into thirds to make small rectangles and cut apart.
3. Place two rectangles together.
4. Secure the two rectangles by folding down one corner.
5. Draw a flower on the top rectangle with a marker.

Production with Specialization

	Output of Rectangular Cards	Output of Triangular Cards
Country A		
Country B		
Total World Output		

Number of Cards after Trade

	Number of Rectangular Cards	Number of Triangular Cards
Country A		
Country B		

Production Without Specialization

	Output of Rectangular Cards	Output of Triangular Cards
Country A		
Country B		
Total World Output		

LESSON DESCRIPTION

Students learn some things about steel and identify a variety of products that are produced with steel. They participate in an activity to help them analyze the costs and benefits of a tariff. Students learn about special-interest groups and consider the arguments people and organizations use to support the imposition of trade barriers.

ECONOMIC CONCEPTS

Trade barriers
Special interest groups
Interdependence
Cost-benefit analysis

OBJECTIVES – Students will:

- Define tariff, trade barriers, interdependence, and special-interest groups.
- Give examples of interdependence.
- Analyze the costs and benefits of policy decisions.
- Explain who gains and who loses when trade barriers are imposed.
- Give examples of special-interest groups

TIME REQUIRED

Two to three class periods

MATERIALS

- Transparency of Visual 9.1
- One copy of Activity 9.1, cut apart to provide one card for each student or pair of students
- Approximately 500 toothpicks

PROCEDURE

1. Write the word "steel" on the board. Ask students the following questions.

    a. What is steel? (*Students may know that steel is a product used in construction. Some may know that it is an alloy made from the combination of several metals.*)
    b. What is steel made from? (*Students probably won't know. Some may know that it is made primarily from a combination of iron and carbon.*)
    c. What is steel used to produce? (*Answers will vary, but may include cars, buildings, and appliances.*)

2. Display a transparency of Visual 9.1. Discuss the following points about steel.

- Steel is an alloy. Alloys are mixtures of two or more metals.
- The primary ingredients in steel are iron and carbon. These ingredients are combined at high temperatures.
- Sir Henry Bessemer received a patent for the original steel-making process in 1856. Steel was used to produce the steel rails on which the "iron horses" traveled.
- The steel-making process has changed a great deal since Sir Bessemer's time, but steel is still a very important factor in the production of many goods. Steel is strong, flexible, and can withstand adverse weather. Steel is used to produce automobile frames, frames for houses, food cans, shipping containers, paint cans, aerosol cans, parts of appliances, water tanks, fuel tanks, bridges, precise surgical instruments used in hospital operating rooms, strong lightweight eyeglass frames, skeletons for commercial buildings, guard rails on highways, signs on highways, underground water and sewer pipes, and rocket motor cases for space shuttles.
- Many people are employed producing products that are made from steel. Many people buy and use products made from steel.

3. Write a headline on the board, "U. S. Places 30% Tariff on Steel," and explain that a **tariff** is a tax on imported goods. Tariffs are barriers to trade. **Trade barriers** are things that make trade less desirable or more difficult. *Note: Lesson 8 in The Wide World of Trade is designed to teach about different types of trade barriers.*

4. Explain that students will participate in an activity in which they identify how a steel tariff – a tax placed on imported steel – would affect various groups of people in the United States and other countries.

5. Distribute a card from Activity 9.1 to each student or to pairs of students.

6. Give each student or pair of students 10 to 30 toothpicks. Tell students to count the number of toothpicks they were given. Explain that the toothpicks represent income that members of the group they represent could spend on goods and services.

7. Have students take turns reading the first paragraph on their cards to the class beginning with cards number 1 and number 2. After reading the first paragraph, students with cards number 3 through 22 should follow the directions given in the second paragraph.

8. When all cards have been read, remind students that each represented a specific group of people. Discuss the following.

    a. How many gave up toothpicks during this activity? (*20*)

    b. How many got additional toothpicks during this activity? (*2*)

9. Explain that the toothpicks given up represent costs and the toothpicks received represent benefits. **Costs** are things sacrificed or given up as the result of a policy or decision (negative result). **Benefits** are things gained or received as a result of a policy or decision (positive result). Many groups incurred costs (gave up toothpicks) but only two groups received benefits (received toothpicks).

10. Point out that costs included paying higher prices for goods and services, earning less income, and doing without goods and services provided by government and by charities. Discuss the following.

    a. What was the cost of the steel tariff to consumers in the United States? (*They had to pay more for products made from steel.*)

    b. What was the cost of the steel tariff to workers at automobile assembly plants in the United States? (*They lost their jobs.*)

    c. What was the cost of the steel tariff to workers at manufacturing companies such as Sony in Japan? (*They lost their jobs.*)

    d. What was the cost of the steel tariff to people in France and other countries who work at steel manufacturing plants? (*They lost their jobs.*)

    e. What was the cost of the steel tariff to people working in Mexico and other countries who produce products made from steel? (*They lost their jobs.*)

    f. What was the cost of the steel tariff to truck drivers and others who transport goods in the United States? (*They lost their jobs or weren't able to work as many hours as before.*)

    g. What was the cost of the steel tariff to people in the United States and other countries who live in communities where there were lay-offs? (*They lost jobs. There were fewer charitable contributions. Government had less tax revenue to provide goods and services in these communities.*)

    h. If people in the United States and in other countries were hurt by the steel tariff, why did Congress impose this policy? (*Answers will vary. Some students might answer that a few groups benefited from the tariff.*)

    i. Who in the United States might favor such a policy? (*large U. S. steel manufacturers, those who work for large U. S. steel manufacturers and their communities*)

11. Explain that often the costs of trade barriers are dispersed widely over large groups of people, and the benefits of trade barriers are received by relatively small groups of people (lots of people gave up a few toothpicks). In the steel example, large

U. S. steel manufacturers and employees of large U. S. steel manufacturers benefited from the policy. They received a lot of toothpicks. Those in the U. S. who produced products made from steel, who consume products made from steel, and so on bore the costs of the tariff. Those in other countries, who worked in the steel industry, produced products made from steel, and those in other countries who consumed steel and products made from steel also bore the costs of the tariff.

12. Read the following scenario to the class, and discuss the questions that follow.

"Members of the high school football team wanted new uniforms and some new equipment. They met with the school principal and convinced him to use money collected as general student fees to provide the uniforms and equipment."

  a. Who benefits from the principal's policy decision? (*members of the football team*) Note: Students may point out that fans will benefit if the team is better equipped and looks better because a better-equipped team may play better and nicer uniforms promote school spirit. However, these are relatively small benefits for fans.
  b. Which is larger, the group of students enrolled at the high school or the group of students who play football? (*group enrolled at high school*)
  c. Who bears the costs of the principal's policy decision? (*All of the students at the high school bear the costs of the policy because all of the students are required to pay the fees*)

13. Explain that in this example, the football team represents a special interest group. A special interest group is a relatively small group of people who lobby for policies or programs. Special interest groups lobby for programs that produce benefits for their group. The cost of these policies is spread among many, many people. In the football example, the team benefits a great deal from the principal's decision. Many other people bear the costs of the principal's decision, and the cost each of these people bears is relatively small.

14. Explain that special interest groups, such as the American Medical Association, the American Association Retired People (AARP), the United Autoworkers, the American Dairy Association, and members of other groups and organizations often lobby congress to influence legislative decisions. Normally, they lobby for programs that will produce great benefits for their group. The costs of their actions are usually spread among many, many people.

15. Point out that in the steel tariff example, large U. S. steel manufacturers and those employed by large U. S. steel manufacturers lobbied Congress for the tariff. This is the group that benefited from the policy that established the tariff. They were the groups that received toothpicks and they received a lot of toothpicks (40).

16. Point out that the costs of the tariff were experienced by many, many other groups of people in the U. S. and in other countries. The costs these people paid were relatively small (2 toothpicks per group).

17. Explain that in other cases, for example, environmental organizations, a relatively small group of people or firms promote a policy that benefits many and imposes costs on a few. For example, pollution control regulations raise the costs for a few large firms; however, millions of people benefit from a cleaner environment.

18. Explain that many groups of people in the United States and in other countries were affected by the steel tariff. This is because people and organizations in the United States and other countries are interdependent. **Economic interdependence** occurs when economic conditions and policies in one community, state, or country affect economic conditions in other communities, states or countries.

19. Write the following sentence stem on the board, "Because of steel tariffs." Ask students to describe examples of interdependence from this activity that would complete the sentence. As students respond, write their responses on the board. Responses would include the following.

    ♦ U. S. workers employed by companies that use steel to produce products were laid off. For example, U. S. automobile workers and construction workers.
    ♦ Workers at companies in Mexico and other countries that produce products made from steel were laid off.
    ♦ Governments in the U. S. and other countries collected less tax revenue because workers were laid off. As a result, governments were able to provide fewer goods and services in the community.
    ♦ Charities in the U. S. and other countries received fewer donations because workers were laid off. As a result, the charities were able to do less good work.
    ♦ Workers in the U. S., Saudi Arabia, Canada, and other countries who produce goods and services used by those associated with the steel industry were laid off. For example, those working for petroleum companies in Saudi Arabia, those working at companies manufacturing car parts

in Canada and those who drove trucks delivering products in the U. S were laid off.

♦ Workers who provide goods and services at stores, restaurants and travel agencies in communities where workers were laid off earned less income and may have lost jobs.

20. Explain that although special interest groups may lobby to impose some type of trade barrier, there are other arguments used to support policies that impose trade barriers. Discuss the following.

♦ One argument in support of trade barriers is national security. In the event of an international crisis or a war, it may be risky for a country to be heavily dependent on foreign suppliers of a product. For example, if the United States didn't have an automobile industry or an aircraft industry, the U. S. would be unable to produce tanks and airplanes in the event of war. Therefore, it might be important to impose trade barriers that protect these industries so that the U. S. is able to produce these products.

♦ Often domestic producers argue that foreign producers have lower wage costs or receive tax concessions or government subsidies. As a result, these foreign producers are able to produce products at lower costs and sell those products at lower prices. Domestic producers want to impose tariffs that will make the price of the foreign product close to the price of the domestic product.

21. Summarize by pointing out that people offer strong arguments for and against imposing trade barriers. Whenever a policy decision is being made regarding a trade barrier, it is important to consider the impact of the policy on domestic consumers, on domestic producers of related products and on foreign producers and consumers. Any policy has far reaching costs and benefits because people, businesses, and organizations in different countries are interdependent.

CLOSURE

Review the key points of the lesson using the following discussion questions.

1. What are trade barriers? (*things that make trade less desirable or more difficult*)

2. When does interdependence occur? (*Interdependence occurs when economic conditions and policies in one area affect*

economic conditions and policies in other areas. This can include economic conditions in one industry affecting people in other industries or economic conditions/policies in one country affecting people in other countries.)

3. What is a benefit? (*A benefit is something gained or received as a result of a policy or decision – a positive result.*)

4. What is a cost? (*A cost is something sacrificed or given up as the result of a policy or decision – negative result.*)

5. Suppose that you spend an additional hour studying for a math test. What is an expected benefit of your decision to study more? (*learning more, doing better on the test*) What is a cost of your decision to study more? (*time that could have been spent doing something else*)

6. What is a special-interest group? (*a relatively small group of people who lobby for policies or programs*)

7. If a special interest group lobbies to impose a trade barrier, which people will most likely benefit from the policy, and which people will most likely bear the costs of the policy (*Members of the special interest group will most likely benefit from the policy, and a large group of other people – consumers, producers of other goods – will bear the costs.*)

8. What arguments are given to support decisions to impose trade barriers? (*national defense and foreign producers receiving subsidies, tax concessions, or paying lower labor costs*)

ASSESSMENT

Have students answer the following questions.

1. Farmers in the European Union lobby for a tariff on U. S. produced wheat. The farmers are successful and the European Union establishes a 15% tariff on U. S. wheat.

    a. Which groups in the U. S. and in European Union countries bear costs as a result of this tariff? What are the costs?
    b. What other businesses might be hurt by the tariff. How are these groups hurt?
    c. Who benefits from this tariff policy?
    d. Who is the special interest group in this example?

2. What is a trade barrier?

3. Your country is considering imposing a tariff on imported automobiles. Take the role of one of the following: a consumer of automobiles in your country, a producer of automobiles in

your country, a producer of automobiles in another country, or a business dependent upon automobile production or consumption such as a tire manufacturer. Write a paragraph explaining the position you would take on this tariff in your role and explain why you would take this position.

EXTENSION

1. Have students locate other products produced with steel. For science, have students conduct research on the basic oxygen steel-making (BOS) process. Have students conduct research about other alloys.

2. Have students conduct research on other products on which the U. S. and other nations have placed either quotas or tariffs. Some examples for the U. S. include peanuts, sugar, rice, wool suits, leather products, and glass products. Students should determine which people, throughout the world, benefit and which people bear the costs of these trade barriers.

1. I represent those who own and operate steel manufacturing plants in the United States. I, along with employees of steel manufacturers in the U. S., lobbied the U. S. Congress for a policy to impose a tariff on steel.	2. I represent workers at U. S. steel manufacturing plants. I, along with owners of steel manufacturing facilities in the U. S., lobbied the U. S. Congress for a policy that would impose a tariff on steel.
3. I represent people who live in Mexico and work for a U. S. company that produces various metal products using U. S. steel. Because of the tariff and increased costs of production, the price of metal products has risen. People are buying fewer metal products. Because the company is selling less, some of my fellow workers and I lose our jobs. *Give a toothpick to the U. S. steel producers and a toothpick to the employees of the U. S. steel manufacturers.*	4. I represent those who work at U. S. automobile assembly plants. Because steel prices are higher, the costs of producing autos have risen, and the prices for autos have risen. U. S. consumers are buying fewer automobiles. As a result, some of my fellow autoworkers and I have lost our jobs. *Give a toothpick to the U. S. steel producers and a toothpick to the employees of the U. S. steel manufacturers.*
5. I represent people who own grocery stores and other businesses in U. S. communities where there are automobile assembly plants. Many people in these communities have lost their jobs because new cars aren't selling very well. Those who are laid off buy fewer groceries and other products from our stores. *Give a toothpick to the U. S. steel producers and a toothpick to the employees of the U. S. steel manufacturers.*	6. I represent people who work for companies in Canada and other countries that sell parts to automobile assembly plants in the United States. The automobile assembly plants are producing fewer cars since the steel tariff, so the automobile assembly plants are buying fewer parts from companies like mine. As a result, these companies don't need as many workers to produce car parts; others and I lose our jobs. *Give a toothpick to the U. S. steel producers and a toothpick to the employees of the U. S. steel manufacturers.*
7. I represent people who live in France and other countries and work for steel manufacturers. Because of the U. S. steel tariff, these companies aren't able to export as much steel to the United States. Because of reduced sales, these companies laid off some of their workers. *Give a toothpick to the U. S. steel producers and a toothpick to the employees of the U. S. steel manufacturers.*	8. I represent workers who are designers and engineers for U. S. auto companies. The price of new cars in the United States has risen because the price of steel has risen. U. S. consumers are buying fewer new cars at the higher prices. As a result, U. S. automobile producers aren't producing as many new cars. Some designers and engineers lose their jobs. *Give a toothpick to the U. S. steel producers and a toothpick to the employees of the U. S. steel manufacturers.*

9. I represent people living in communities where workers have been laid off because of the steel tariff or because of rising steel prices. People who aren't working don't pay as much tax to governments. As a result, governments don't have money for various projects such as road and bridge improvement. *Give a toothpick to the U. S. steel producers and a toothpick to the employees of the U. S. steel manufacturers.*	10. I represent owners of cafés and other small businesses located near steel companies in France and other countries. Steelworkers in these communities have lost their jobs. Because they aren't working, people in the communities don't eat at the café or buy from other businesses as often as they used to. I, and others who own cafés and businesses, earn less income. *Give a toothpick to the U. S. steel producers and a toothpick to the employees of the U. S. steel manufacturers.*
11. I represent those who live in Japan and work for corporations, such as Sony, that sell many products in other countries. Because of lay-offs in the automobile industry, construction industry, and other related businesses in the United States and other countries, people in the United States and other countries are buying fewer Sony products. As a result, I, and other workers at Sony and corporations like Sony have lost our jobs. *Give a toothpick to the U. S. steel producers and a toothpick to the employees of the U. S. steel manufacturers.*	12. I represent those who live in Saudi Arabia and other countries that export petroleum. Factories in the U. S. and other countries are producing less because of increased steel prices. As a result, they are buying less petroleum and fewer petroleum products used to operate the factories and used in production. I and other workers at petroleum companies in Saudi Arabia and other countries have lost our jobs. *Give a toothpick to the U. S. steel producers and a toothpick to the employees of the U. S. steel manufacturers.*
13. I represent owners of construction companies in the United States. These companies buy steel and use it to produce buildings and other structures. Because of the steel tariff, the price of steel has gone up. It costs us more to produce buildings and other structures. Our profits are reduced. *Give a toothpick to the U. S. steel producers and a toothpick to the employees of the U. S. steel manufacturers.*	14. I represent people who work for construction companies in the U. S. Because of the steel tariff, the price of steel has risen, meaning that it costs more for the construction companies to build things. As a result, the companies are building fewer things and fewer workers are needed. I, and others, lose our jobs. *Give a toothpick to the U. S. steel producers and a toothpick to the employees of the U. S. steel manufacturers.*

The Wide World of Trade © National Council on Economic Education, New York, NY

15. I represent U. S. consumers. U. S. consumers buy products made from steel, such as eyeglass frames, cars, appliances, cans of food, cans of paint, and products in aerosol cans. Because the price of steel has risen, the cost of producing these products has risen, and the prices of these products have risen. *Give a toothpick to the U. S. steel producers and a toothpick to the employees of the U. S. steel manufacturers.*	16. I represent travel agents in communities where workers have lost jobs. Because people have less income, they aren't planning as many trips. Because other travel agents and I don't have as many customers, we don't earn as much. *Give a toothpick to the U. S. steel producers and a toothpick to the employees of the U. S. steel manufacturers.*
17. I represent truck drivers in the U. S. We drive trucks that carry new automobiles, equipment, appliances, and other products made from steel. Because of the steel tariff and rising steel prices people are buying fewer new cars, less equipment, and so on. Fewer of these products are being transported. Trucking companies don't need as many drivers. Some truckers lose their jobs. Some work fewer hours. *Give a toothpick to the U. S. steel producers and a toothpick to the employees of the U. S. steel manufacturers.*	18. I represent people who operate charitable organizations in communities where people have lost jobs as a result of the steel tariff and higher steel prices. These organizations rely on donations from members of the community. The money collected is used to help poor people who need food and clothing. Many people in these communities have been laid-off from their jobs at an automobile assembly plant. Because they aren't working, they aren't making contributions to charity and we aren't able to help as many people. *Give a toothpick to the U. S. steel producers and a toothpick to the employees of the U. S. steel manufacturers.*

- ◆ Steel is an alloy.

- ◆ Steel is made primarily from iron and carbon.

- ◆ Steel was important to the development of the railway system in the U. S.

- ◆ Today steel is used to produce many different products.

- ◆ Many people are employed producing products made from steel.

- ◆ Many people buy products that are made from steel.

LESSON DESCRIPTION

In this lesson, students imagine a visit to the Mall of the World, a large international mall with shops that are owned and operated by people in other countries. Students choose items to eat at The Wide World of Taste, an international food court. Prices are stated in the currencies used by the countries represented, and students must use exchange rates to determine how much their lunches will cost. Students then learn about appreciation and depreciation of currencies.

ECONOMIC CONCEPTS

Foreign exchange
Exchange rate
Currency appreciation
Currency depreciation

OBJECTIVES – Students will:

- Define foreign exchange, exchange rate, appreciation, and depreciation.
- Compute currency equivalents using exchange rates.
- Explain whether currencies appreciate or depreciate, given exchange rate changes.
- Describe the effect of a change in exchange rates on amounts spent on foreign goods and services.

TIME REQUIRED

One class period

MATERIALS

- Transparencies of Visuals 10.1 and 10.2
- One copy of Activity 10.1
- Two copies of 10.2 for each student
- Calculators (optional)

PROCEDURE

1. Ask students if they've heard about the Mall of America in Minnesota. Explain that it is one of the largest malls in the world with over 500 stores employing over 12,000 people. The mall attracts more visitors annually than Walt Disney World®, Graceland, and the Grand Canyon combined.

2. Tell the class to imagine that a larger mall, the Mall of the World, has been created in their community with over 1000 shops and entertainment facilities. These shops are owned and operated by people and businesses from around the world. Best of all, there is an international food court, The Wide World of Taste, with delicious foods from around the world.

3.   Explain that students will select a lunch at the international food court. They may spend $10.00. Display Visual 10.1 and explain that the list contains their choices. Allow time for students to develop a list of items that they'd prefer to eat and drink.

4.   Give students a copy of Activity 10.1 and tell them to place a checkmark next to the items that they'd like to purchase for lunch. Students will notice that the items are not priced in dollars, but tell them to go ahead and check the items that they want.

5.   Remind students that this is a unique mall with shops that are owned and operated by people from other countries. The owners and operators want to be paid in their currencies. This is true in all stores at the mall. Most countries create their own currency for use as money. In this case, there are five different currencies that may be required to buy lunch: Australian dollars, Chinese yuan, European Union euros, Mexican pesos, and Egyptian pounds. These currencies are foreign exchange to U.S. citizens. Define **foreign exchange** as all currencies other than the domestic currency in a specific country.

6.   Have students define their problem. (*The prices are not in U.S. dollars, so they don't know the price or what and how much they can afford.*)

7.   Announce that a currency exchange bank is located at the Mall of the World, so they can exchange their U.S. dollars for the currencies that they need to buy lunch.

8.   Display Visual 10.2, explaining that the currency exchange bank has posted these exchange rates. Define **exchange rate** as the price of one nation's currency in terms of another nation's currency. In this case, all currencies are priced in terms of U.S. dollars. Point out the following.

   ▪ One U.S. dollar will buy 1.8 Australian dollars.
   ▪ One U.S. dollar will buy .90 European Union euros.
   ▪ One U.S. dollar will buy 8.0 Chinese yuan.
   ▪ One U.S. dollar will buy 10.2 Mexican pesos.
   ▪ One U.S. dollar will buy 4.6 Egyptian pounds.

9.   Give a copy of Activity 10.2 to each student and assign. Distribute calculators (optional). Demonstrate computation on the board using the following example.

   ▪ Assume that Lindsey purchases three Tijuana Tacos.
   ▪ The price is 15.30 pesos, so the amount she would spend in pesos would be 45.90 pesos (15.30 x 3 = 45.90).

- The exchange rate is one U.S. dollar equals 10.2 Mexican pesos (1 USD = 10.2 MXN).
- The total amount of U.S. dollars required to purchase the three tacos would be 45.90 divided by 10.2, or 4.50 USD.

10. Have students work individually or in pairs to complete their worksheets. When finished, ask how many students could purchase their lunch with $10.

11. Give another copy of Activity 10.2 to each student. Tell students to alter their purchases to spend $10 (or as close to $10 as they can get without exceeding $10). When everyone has finished, have a few students share what they chose and how much the lunches cost.

12. Discuss the following.

   a. What is the price of an egg roll in yuan? (*6 CNY*)
   b. What is the price of an egg roll in U.S. dollars? (*$.75 = 6/8*)
   c. Assume that the exchange rate changed from 1 USD = 8 CNY to 1 USD = 12 CNY. What is the price of an egg roll with the new exchange rate? (*$.50 = 6/12*)
   d. Why have egg rolls become less expensive in terms of U.S. dollars. (*The U.S. dollar can now purchase more Chinese yuan, so the customer can purchase more egg rolls.*)

13. Point out that, in this example, the U.S. dollar has appreciated relative to the Chinese yuan, and the Chinese yuan has depreciated relative to the U.S. dollar. Explain that **appreciation** of a currency means that people can exchange that currency for more of another currency. **Depreciation** of a currency means that people can exchange that currency for less of another currency.

   a. How has the U.S. dollar appreciated relative to the Chinese yuan? (*One dollar will now buy more CNY – 12 CNY instead of 8 CNY.*)
   b. How has the Chinese yuan depreciated relative to the U.S. dollar? (*8 CNY could purchase one USD before the exchange rate change. After the rate change, 8 CNY will only purchase .75 USD.*)
   c. If the exchange rate between the U.S. dollar and the Egyptian pound changed from 1 USD = 4.6 EGP to 1 USD = 2.76 EGP, has the U.S. dollar appreciated or depreciated relative to the EGP? Why? (*The U.S. dollar has depreciated relative to the Egyptian pound because one dollar will not buy as many Egyptian pounds.*)
   d. If prices of Egyptian drinks remained the same, will customers be able to buy more or fewer drinks with a fixed amount of U.S. dollars? (*Fewer. The dollars aren't worth as much in Egyptian pounds.*)

14. Explain that exchange rates between currencies fluctuate all the time. Students can find current exchange rates on the Internet at *http://www.oanda.com/convert/classic/*.

CLOSURE

Review the key points of the lesson using the following discussion questions.

1. Why can't U.S. citizens use their U.S. dollars to pay for goods and services in other countries? (*People in other countries prefer to be paid in their currencies.*)

2. If a group of U.S. citizens wanted to pay for a tour in Paris, France, what must the citizens do? (*They must convert their U.S. dollars into European Union euros.*)

3. What is an exchange rate? (*the price of one nation's currency in terms of another nation's currency*)

4. If 1 USD = 10.2 MXN and 1 USD = .90 EUR, what is the exchange rate between Mexican pesos and European Union euros? (*10.2 MXN = .90 EUR*)

5. If the exchange rate between the Mexican peso and the European Union euro changed from 10.2 MXN = .90 EUR to 10.2 MXN = 1.00 EUR, has the peso appreciated or depreciated relative to the euro? (*It has appreciated relative to the euro.*) What has happened to the euro? (*It has depreciated relative to the Mexican peso.*)

6. If the exchange rate between the Australian dollar and the Chinese yuan changed from 1.8 AUD = 4.6 EGP to 1.8 AUD = 3.7 EGP, has the Australian dollar appreciated or depreciated relative to the Chinese yuan? Why? (*It has depreciated because one Australian dollar will not buy as many Egyptian pounds.*) What has happened to the Egyptian pound? (*It has appreciated relative to the Australian dollar because it now only takes 3.6 EGP instead of 4.6 EGP to buy 1.8 Australian dollars.*)

ASSESSMENT

1. If people in Mexico want to buy cotton from Egypt, then:
   a. They must exchange Egyptian pounds for Mexican pesos.
   b. 4.6 Egyptian pounds for 10.2 Mexican pesos would be better than 5.6 Egyptian pounds.
   c. They must exchange Mexican pesos for Egyptian pounds. *
   d. They will be better off if the Egyptian pound appreciates relative to the Mexican peso.

2. If the exchange rate between U.S. dollars and Australian dollars changes from 1 USD = 1.8 AUD to 1USD = 1.5 AUD, then:
    a. The U.S. dollar has appreciated relative to the Australian dollar.
    b. The Australian dollar has appreciated relative to the U.S. dollar. *
    c. The Australian dollar has depreciated relative to the U.S. dollar.
    d. Australian goods will be cheaper to Americans.

3. (Short answer) Describe what would happen to a family's expenses for a trip to Europe if the U.S. dollar depreciated relative to the European Union euro. Explain your answer.

EXTENSION

Give students the following shopping list. Tell them to go to the Internet and use a currency converter (one may be found at *http://www.oanda.com/convert/classic*) to determine the total cost of the items.

Japanese Sony Playstation®2	24,000 Japanese yen
Brazilian soccer ball	90 Brazilian reals
Chinese silk purse	249 Chinese yuan
Swiss snow ski goggles	56 Swiss francs
French perfume	39 European Union euros
Korean athletic shoes	102,170 South-Korean won
Kenyan carved elephant	2,791 Kenyan shilling
Turkish brass bracelet	19,764 Turkish lira
Australian gold earrings	323 Australian dollars

The Wide World of Taste

Australian Appetizers

Down Under Cheese Hoppers	4.50 dollars
Great Barrier Reef Finger Foods	2.70 dollars
Outback Croc Pot Stickers	1.80 dollars
Sydney Sheep Sizzlers	3.60 dollars

CHINESE CHOW

GREAT WALL EGG ROLL	6 YUAN
MANDARIN GARLIC CHICKEN	20 YUAN
SZECHWAN SPICY SHRIMP	26 YUAN
SHANGHAIED FRIED RICE	14 YUAN

Continental Cuisine

French Onion Soup	1.80 euros
Greek Salad	2.52 euros
German Brats (best of the wurst)	2.97 euros
Luck of the Irish Stew	2.25 euros
Italian Spaghetti and Meatballs	2.70 euros
Spanish Flan (a rich custard)	1.98 euros
Belgian Chocolates	3.60 euros
Finnish Cranberry Drink	1.62 euros

MEXICAN MOUTHFULS

TIJUANA TACO	15.30 PESOS
CHIHUAHUA ENCHILADA	18.36 PESOS
BURRITO YUCATAN	22.44 PESOS
FAJITAS DE FRANCISCO	35.70 PESOS
REFRIED BEANS DE GUERRERO	8.16 PESOS
NACHOS DE TABASCO	20.40 PESOS

Egyptian Elixirs

Cold Camel Cairo Coffee	6.90 pounds
Luscious Luxor Lemonade	9.20 pounds
Mango Juice Masterpiece	10.35 pounds
Suez-Sinai Soda	5.75 pounds

Instructions:

1. Indicate the quantity of each item that you **want** to buy.
2. Multiply the quantity by the price and enter the total amount that would be spent in the foreign currency.
3. Using the exchange rate at the currency exchange bank, convert to the amount in U.S. dollars.
4. Calculate the total U.S. dollar cost of your lunch.

Item	Quantity	Price	Total amount in foreign currency	Amount in USD ($)
Down Under Cheese Hoppers		4.50 AUD		
Great Barrier Reef Finger Foods		2.70 AUD		
Outback Croc Pot Stickers		1.80 AUD		
Sydney Sheep Sizzlers		3.60 AUD		
GREAT WALL EGG ROLL		**6 CYN**		
MANDARIN GARLIC CHICKEN		**20 CYN**		
SZECHWAN SPICY SHRIMP		**26 CYN**		
SHANGHAIED FRIED RICE		**14 CYN**		
French Onion Soup		1.80 EUR		
Greek Salad		2.52 EUR		
German Brats (best of the wurst)		2.97 EUR		
Luck of the Irish Stew		2.25 EUR		
Italian Spaghetti and Meatballs		2.70 EUR		
Spanish Flan (a rich custard!)		1.98 EUR		
Belgian Chocolates		3.60 EUR		
Finnish Cranberry Drink		1.62 EUR		
TIJUANA TACO		15.30 MXN		
CHIHUAHUA ENCHILADA		18.36 MXN		
BURRITO YUCATAN		22.44 MXN		
FAJITAS DE FRANCISCO		35.70 MXN		
REFRIED BEANS DE GUERRERO		8.16 MXN		
NACHOS DE TABASCO		20.40 MXN		
Cold Camel Cairo Coffee		6.90 EGP		
Luscious Luxor Lemonade		9.20 EGP		
Mango Juice Masterpiece		10.35 EGP		
Suez-Sinai Soda		5.75 EGP		
TOTAL COST OF LUNCH IN U.S. DOLLARS				

Australian Appetizers

Down Under Cheese Hoppers
Great Barrier Reef Finger Foods
Outback Croc Pot Stickers
Sydney Sheep Sizzlers

CHINESE CHOW

GREAT WALL EGG ROLL
MANDARIN GARLIC CHICKEN
SZECHWAN SPICY SHRIMP
SHANGHAIED FRIED RICE

Continental Cuisine

French Onion Soup
Greek Salad
German Brats (best of the wurst)
Luck of the Irish Stew
Italian Spaghetti and Meatballs
Spanish Flan (a rich custard)
Belgian Chocolates
Finnish Cranberry Drink

MEXICAN MOUTHFULS

TIJUANA TACO
CHIHUAHUA ENCHILADA
BURRITO YUCATAN
FAJITAS DE FRANCISCO
REFRIED BEANS DE GUERRERO
NACHOS DE TABASCO

Egyptian Elixirs

Cold Camel Cairo Coffee
Luscious Luxor Lemonade
Mango Juice Masterpiece
Suez-Sinai Soda

The Mall of the World Currency Bank

Exchange Rates

1 USD = 1.8 AUD

1 USD = 8.0 CYN

1 USD = .90 EUR

1 USD = 10.2 MXN

1 USD = 4.6 EGP

USD = U.S. dollar
AUD = Australian dollar
CYN = Chinese Yuan
EUR = European euro
MXN = Mexican peso
EGP = Egyptian pound

LESSON DESCRIPTION

After listing some of their own buying and selling activities, students recognize that most people and families are both buyers and sellers who make exchanges in different kinds of markets. The relationship between output markets for goods and services and input markets for productive resources is shown in the simplest picture or model of a market economy – the circular flow of income.

Buying and selling goods and services from or to people and organizations in other countries is not really different from the market exchanges that are shown in the circular flow model, except for the complication of using different national currencies. After completing a matching activity that reviews the different names for money in different nations, the class looks at a diagram to understand why people in one country would want to buy currency from another country and other people would want to sell it. This explains why currency exchange markets for international currencies exist.

ECONOMIC CONCEPTS

Markets
Circular flow
International trade
Imports
Exports
Currency exchange

OBJECTIVES – Students will:

- Define currency exchange, market, import, and export.
- Identify examples of buying and selling activities in markets.
- Explain that most people and families are buyers in some markets and sellers in others.
- Explain how households and firms interact in a market economy, using a simple circular flow model.
- Compare buying and selling goods and services to and from people and organizations in another nation to buying and selling that takes place within a single nation.

TIME REQUIRED

One or two class periods

MATERIALS

- Copy of Activities 11.1 - 11.4 for each student
- Transparencies of Activity 11.1 and Visuals 11.1 - 11.3
- World atlases

PROCEDURE

1. Have students make a list of all the goods and services they have purchased in the last week and indicate next to each item where or from whom they purchased it.

2. Have students share examples of goods and services they have listed. Record their answers on the board or a transparency in a column labeled "Buyer." Discuss the following.

   a. Give examples of places from which some of these goods and services were purchased. (*shopping malls, movie theatres, video stores, fast food restaurants, and grocery stores*)
   b. Can you give examples of exchanges you made with friends during the week? (*Answers will vary.*)

3. Write "market" on the board, and ask students if all the purchases on their lists were made in a market. (*Students may think that some of their purchases were made in such informal settings – especially if some of the purchases or trades were made with friends or family members in somebody's home, at school, or just walking down the street – that there was no market involved.*)

4. Explain that a **market** exists any time buyers and sellers interact to make voluntary exchanges of goods and services for money or for other goods and services. That means that any buying and selling, including trading between friends and family, establishes a market. Ask the students if they or family members have ever participated in any of the following markets – flea market, E-bay™, shop from catalogs, order something advertised on television, garage sale, answered a "want ad" from the newspaper for a job, or stock market.

5. Explain that some markets are huge and highly organized, involving millions of buyers and sellers from all over the world, such as the markets for stocks and bonds issued by large corporations. Other markets, such as local flea markets, are much smaller and more informal. Point out that sometimes trading takes place where there are no stores or even stalls for sellers to display their wares. In all of these cases, however, the buying, selling, and trading are market transactions.

6. Explain that in some cases buyers and sellers never meet in person – in fact, most buying and selling of stocks and bonds is done this way, over the telephone or Internet, through "middlemen" called brokers.

7. Point out that the list on the board provides examples of times when students were buyers in markets over the last week. Now

ask them to list any cases in which they, or their parents, sold something in a market. (*While some students or parents may have sold or traded a good over the past week, many may not.*)

8.   After allowing a few minutes for students to think about and list anything they have sold or traded, ask for a show of hands from any students who did a particular job for pay (including any allowance they receive from their parents).

9.   Point out that any of those jobs that were done for pay, and whatever jobs their parents have, represent the sale of their labor services to an employer. Over a person's lifetime, the labor market is where most people sell the most valuable resource they own, and by doing so earn most of their income.

10. Have students add any jobs they or their parents did for pay to the list of things they sold over the past week. On the board or a transparency, make a class list of some of these items in a column labeled "Seller."

11. Display Visual 11.1 and distribute a copy of Activity 11.1 to each student. Point out that this picture represents the flows of resources, goods and services and money payments to show how buyers and sellers interact in a market economy. The diagram is called the **circular flow**. Explain the following.

   ♦   In a market economy, households and businesses interact in two different kinds of markets, product (output) markets and factor (resource) markets.
   ♦   Businesses sell goods and services to consumers in product (output) markets. For example, grocery stores, department stores, video stores, movie theatres and restaurants sell goods and services to households. Point out the box labeled "Goods and Services" on the transparency. Tell students to write "Goods and Services" in the box below "Product Markets" on their diagrams. Using a transparency pen, trace the dotted line from the "Businesses" box to the "Goods and Services" box. Tell students to draw a dotted line from the "Businesses" box to the "Goods and Services" box on their diagram.
   ♦   Households are people, like the students and their families, who buy goods and services. Trace the dotted line from the "Goods and Services" box to the "Households" box on the transparency. Tell students to draw a dotted line from the "Goods and Services" box to the "Households" box on their diagram.
   ♦   Households also sell labor and other resources (including natural resources, capital, and entrepreneurship) to businesses in the factor (resource) markets. Point out the "Productive Resources " box on the transparency. Tell

students to write "Productive Resources" in the box above "Factor Markets" on their diagram. Trace the dotted line from the "Households" box to the "Productive Resources" box on the diagram. Tell students to draw a dotted line from the "Households" box to the "Productive Resources" box on their diagram.

♦ Refer students to the list in the "Seller" column on the board for examples of people in households selling resources.

♦ Businesses buy resources from households and use the resources to produce goods and services. Trace the dotted line from the "Productive Resources" box to the "Businesses" box on the diagram. Tell students to draw a dotted line from the "Productive Resources" box to the "Businesses" box on their diagram.

♦ Businesses must pay for the resources that they buy from households. For example, businesses pay wages and salaries for labor (human resources). Note: The payments firms make for capital goods, natural resources, and entrepreneurial ability are called interest, rent, and profit respectively.

♦ The payments businesses make are income for households. **Income** is the payment households earn for selling the resources they own in markets. Trace the two solid lines from the "Businesses" box to the "Households" box on the transparency. Tell students to draw two, similar solid lines from the "Businesses" box to the "Households" box.

♦ Households spend income on goods and services. This income is revenue (sales dollars) for businesses. Trace the two, solid lines from the "Households" box to the "Businesses" box on the transparency. Tell students to draw two, solid lines from the "Households" box to the "Businesses" box.

♦ The circular flow chart is the simplest model of a market economy or market system, showing how buyers and sellers interact. Households are buyers of goods and services and sellers of productive resources. Businesses buy productive resources and sell goods and services.

12. Point out that the circular flow model in Visual 11.1 is an extremely simple model of a market economy because it leaves out some important parts of the real economy. In particular, note that the government is neither a household nor a business and is not shown here. If government were shown it would make the chart much more complicated because government spending, taxing, and laws and regulations affect households, businesses, product markets, and the markets for inputs or productive resources. Those are topics for another day and another lesson, however.

13. Explain that the circular flow chart also doesn't show buying and
     selling that involves people and businesses from other countries.
     Point out that exchange among people and organizations in
     other countries is called **international trade**.

14. Have students make a list of goods and services that U.S.
     consumers purchase from other countries. Allow them to check
     labels on clothes they are wearing or other items in the room as
     they write this list. If necessary, offer hints or remind them to
     include foreign automobiles, electronic goods, and foods grown
     in other countries, such as coffee, tea, and cocoa beans.

15. After allowing time for students to work, have them name items
     on their lists. Record their examples on the board to create a
     class list of these items in a column titled "Purchased from Other
     Countries."

16. Have students make a list of goods and services that U.S.
     producers sell to consumers and companies from other
     countries. If students have difficulty with this list, offer the
     following hints.

     ♦ Think of some agricultural products (such as wheat, corn,
        and soybeans) that we grow in the United States.
     ♦ Think of some entertainment products that we produce in the
        United States. (movie and music CDs, best-selling novels
        and books)
     ♦ Think of some kinds of automobiles (especially SUVs,
        minivans, and pickup trucks) that we produce in the United
        States.
     ♦ Think of some products we produce for the airline industry.
        (large commercial jets)

17. After allowing time for students to work, have them name items
     on their lists. Record their examples on the board to create a
     class list of these items in a column titled "Sold to Other
     Countries."

18. Define **imports** as goods and services bought from individuals
     and organizations in other countries, and **exports** as goods and
     services sold to individuals and organizations in other countries.
     Add those terms, in parentheses, to the column headings
     "Purchased from" and "Sold to," respectively.

19. Display Visual 11.2. Briefly compare the items on the visual to
     the lists students developed.

20. Note that in most ways, international trade is simply more of the
     buying and selling involving households and firms, as shown in
     the circular flow model in Visual 11.1. Of course, with

international trade, the households and businesses are located in different nations around the world.

21. Explain that another key difference between exchange within a nation and international trade is that different nations use different currencies.

22. Explain that because countries use different currencies, when people engage in international trade, currency exchange must take place. **Currency exchange** involves trading one nation's currency for another. This type of exchange takes place in currency exchange markets. This means, for example, that if people from the United States want to buy products from Japan, they must trade some U.S. dollars for Japanese yen. Discuss the following.

a. If you went to a restaurant near your home for dinner, would the owner let you pay with currency from Japan? (*No.*) Why not? (*The restaurant owner can't use Japanese currency to buy things or to pay his employees.*)
b. Why wouldn't you want your parents to pay your allowance in Mexican currency? (*You couldn't spend it at the mall, movie theatre, or restaurants near where you live.*)

23. Point out that just as restaurant owners and households in the U. S. expect to be paid in U. S. dollars, people and businesses in other countries expect to receive payment in their countries' currencies.

24. Distribute a copy of Activity 11.2 to each student. Review the directions and remind students that they will use four of the currency names more than one time as they match. Tell students that they may use world atlases to help them complete this activity.

25. Allow time for students to match the names of the national currencies with the countries. Review the correct answers:

Argentina	Peso
Australia	Dollar
Brazil	Real
Canada	Dollar
China	Yuan
Egypt	Pound
France	Euro (formerly Franc)
Germany	Euro (formerly Mark)
Greece	Drachma
India	Rupee
Italy	Euro (formerly Lira)
Japan	Yen

Mexico	Peso
Poland	Zloty
Russia	Ruble
Saudi Arabia	Riyal
South Korea	Won
Turkey	Lira
United Kingdom	Pound
United States	Dollar

26. Point out that, although many countries use the same names for their currencies, that does not always mean the currencies actually look the same or are worth the same amount (for example, in 2002 it took more than one Canadian or Australian dollar to buy one U.S. dollar).

27. Explain that other countries may choose to use the same currency. For example in 2002, many European nations began to use the same currency, the euro, partly to make it easier for people to travel throughout that region and for people and businesses to trade with each other.

28. Display Visual 11.3 and distribute a copy of Activity 11. 3 to each student. Tell students that this diagram will help explain how people and organizations in one country are able to buy goods and services in another even though different currencies are involved.

   ♦ People and organizations in the United States who want to buy Japanese goods and services must pay for those goods with Japanese yen. To do that, they must exchange dollars for yen in the currency exchange markets. Trace the arrow from the "United States People and Organizations" box to the "Currency Exchange Markets" box. Tell students to draw this arrow on their diagram and to add dollar signs as shown on the transparency. Trace the line from the "Currency Exchange Markets" box to the "United States People and Organizations" box. Tell students to draw this arrow on their diagram and to add yen symbols as shown on the transparency.

   ♦ When they have completed the currency exchange, they can exchange yen for the Japanese goods and services they want to buy. Trace the line from the "United States People and Organizations" box to the "Goods and Services Markets" box on the diagram. Tell students to draw this arrow on their diagram and to add the yen symbols as shown on the transparency. Trace the arrow from the "Goods and Services Markets" box to the "United States People and Organizations" box on the diagram. Tell students to draw this arrow on their diagram and to write the words "Japanese goods and services."

♦ People and organizations in Japan who want to buy U. S. goods and services must pay for those goods and services with U. S. dollars. To do that, they must exchange yen for dollars in the currency exchange markets. Trace the arrow from the "Japanese People and Organizations" box to the "Currency Exchange Markets" box on the transparency. Tell students to draw this arrow on their diagram, and to add the yen symbols as shown on the transparency. Trace the arrow from the "Currency Exchange Markets" box to the "Japanese People and Organizations" box on the transparency. Tell students to draw this arrow on their diagram and to add dollar signs as shown on the transparency.

♦ When they have completed the currency exchange, they can exchange the dollars for the U. S. goods and services they want to buy. Trace the arrow from the "Japanese People and Organizations" box to the "Goods and Services Markets" box on the diagram. Tell students to draw this arrow on their diagram and to add dollar signs as shown on the transparency. Trace the arrow from the "Goods and Services Markets" box to the "Japanese People and Organizations" box on the diagram. Tell students to draw this arrow on their diagram and to write "U. S. goods and services" as shown on the transparency.

Note: Some students may comment that when their parents bought a new car that was produced in another country, they paid for it with dollars. In those cases, either the dealership that bought the car from the foreign manufacturer had already paid for the car in the foreign currency, or the dollars will eventually be converted into the foreign currency. After all, a foreign car manufacturer can't pay its workers or other expenses with dollars. So one way or another, buyers of goods and services made in another country also create a demand for the currency of that nation.

29. Explain that when people and organizations from one country buy another country's currency, they do it by selling currency from their own county. For example, when someone from the United States buys yen to buy a car made in Japan, they do that by selling dollars in exchange for the yen. They can do that because there are people and businesses in Japan who want to get dollars, either to buy goods and services produced in the United States or to invest in the United States. Those are the people or firms who will sell yen for dollars.

30. Explain that investors, not just consumers, buy and sell currencies. If a person or firm wants to invest in another country, perhaps by buying or building factories or stores there or by purchasing bonds and other financial securities that are

issued in that country, they must pay for those investments in
the other nation's currency.

31. Explain that, in order to make the investments, the investor will
    sell or exchange his or her own nation's currency. Display
    Visual 11.3 again and explain the following.

    ♦ A U.S. bank is an organization in the United States. If the
      bank wants to buy a building and open a branch office in
      Tokyo, it will buy yen and pay for those yen with U.S. dollars.
    ♦ The bank will use the yen to buy a building and equipment
      and hire workers in Japan.
    ♦ A Japanese automobile company is an organization in
      Japan. If the company decides to build a factory in the
      United States it will buy dollars with yen.
    ♦ The automobile company will use the dollars to build the
      factory, buy equipment, and hire workers.

32. Emphasize that although international trade is more complicated
    than trading that takes place between people who live in the
    same nation because it involves the additional step of currency
    exchange, fundamentally it is the same kind of buying and
    selling in markets that students and other people engage in
    every day.

33. Remind students that many of the goods and services
    consumed in the United States today are produced in other
    countries, and many of the goods and services produced in the
    United States are sold in other countries. Currency exchange
    markets (also known as foreign exchange markets), where the
    currencies for nations from all over the world are traded, make it
    much easier for the international trading of goods and services
    to take place.

CLOSURE

Review the key points of the lesson using the following discussion
questions.

1. When do markets exist? (*whenever buyers and sellers interact*)

2. Give an example of people or organizations that are buyers of
   some things and sellers of other things. (*Family members sell
   human resources in factor markets to earn income; family
   members buy goods and services in product markets.*)

3. What does the circular flow model illustrate? (*movement of
   goods, services, resources, and money in the economy*)

4. Why do people and organizations in one country buy currency from another country? (*to buy goods and services produced in the other country or to make investments in the other country*)

5. What do people and organizations in one country sell in order to buy currency from another country? (*their country's currency*)

6. Where does currency exchange take place? (*in currency exchange markets*)

7. How is trade within a country like trade with other countries? (*In both cases there are people who want to sell goods, services, and resources and people who want to buy goods, services and resources. Both involve the use of currency.*)

8. How is trade within a country different from trade with other countries? (*Trade with other countries requires currency exchange,*)

9. What is currency exchange? (*buying one country's currency with another country's currency*)

ASSESSMENT

1. Have students write an essay describing what would happen if each state issued its own money, and purchases made in each state could only be made using the money from that state.

2. Give students a copy of activity 11.4. Read the following scenario and have students label the boxes and draw and label arrows on the diagram to show the exchanges that must take place.

   People in Germany want to buy goods and services from people in Japan. People in Japan want to buy goods and services from people in Germany. The Japanese currency is yen (¥). The German currency is euros (€). On the diagram, show the exchanges that must take place.

EXTENSION

Teach lesson 10 from *The Wide World of Trade*.

Money Payments (Sales Dollars)

PRODUCT MARKETS

HOUSEHOLDS

BUSINESSES

FACTOR MARKETS

Money Income Payments (Rents, Interest,
Wages and Salaries, and Profits)

Do you know the name of the money used in countries from around the world? Write the name of the currency in the blank after each country, using the currencies listed in the far right column.

Some countries use the same name for their money, so you will use four of the currency names more than one time.

Country		Currency
Argentina	_____	Dollar
Australia	_____	Drachma
Brazil	_____	Euro
Canada	_____	Lira
China	_____	Peso
Egypt	_____	Pound
France	_____	Real
Germany	_____	Riyal
Greece	_____	Ruble
India	_____	Rupee
Italy	_____	Won
Japan	_____	Yen
Mexico	_____	Yuan
Poland	_____	Zloty
Russia	_____	
Saudi Arabia	_____	
South Korea	_____	
Turkey	_____	
United Kingdom	_____	
United States	_____	

Japanese People and Organizations

Currency Exchange Markets		Goods and Services Markets

United States People and Organizations

Japanese People
and Organizations

Currency
Exchange
Markets

Goods and
Services
Markets

People and
Organizations

The Circular Flow of Productive Resources, Goods and Services, and Money Payments

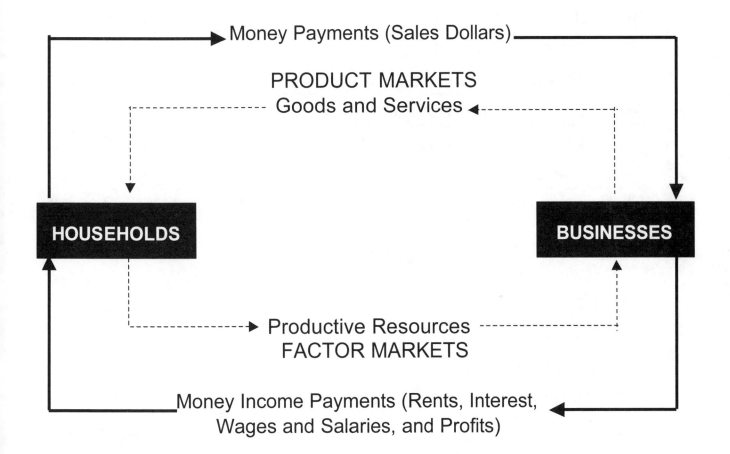

Money Payments (Sales Dollars)

PRODUCT MARKETS
Goods and Services

HOUSEHOLDS

BUSINESSES

Productive Resources
FACTOR MARKETS

Money Income Payments (Rents, Interest, Wages and Salaries, and Profits)

Top Ten U.S. Imports*

Computer accessories	$15,591
Crude oil	14,220
Pharmaceutical preparations	9,266
Apparel, household goods-cotton	8,449
Other household goods	7,388
Semiconductors	6,622
Apparel, textiles, nonwool or cotton	5,799
Telecommunications equipment	5,596
TV's, VCR's, etc	5,468
Electric apparatus	5,397

Top Ten U.S. Exports*

Semiconductors	$10,303
Computer accessories	7,305
Civilian aircraft	6,523
Telecommunications equipment	6,044
Electric apparatus	5,270
Pharmaceutical preparations	3,948
Medicinal equipment	3,526
Plastic materials	3,341
Chemicals-organic	3,171
Measuring, testing, control instruments	3,171

* in millions of dollars

Source: Bureau of the Census, Bureau of Economic Analysis. *U.S. International trade in goods and services.* March 2002. Exhibit 7 and 8. Exports of Goods and Imports of Goods by End-Use Category and Commodity. http://www.bea.gov/bea/newsrel/trad0302.xls

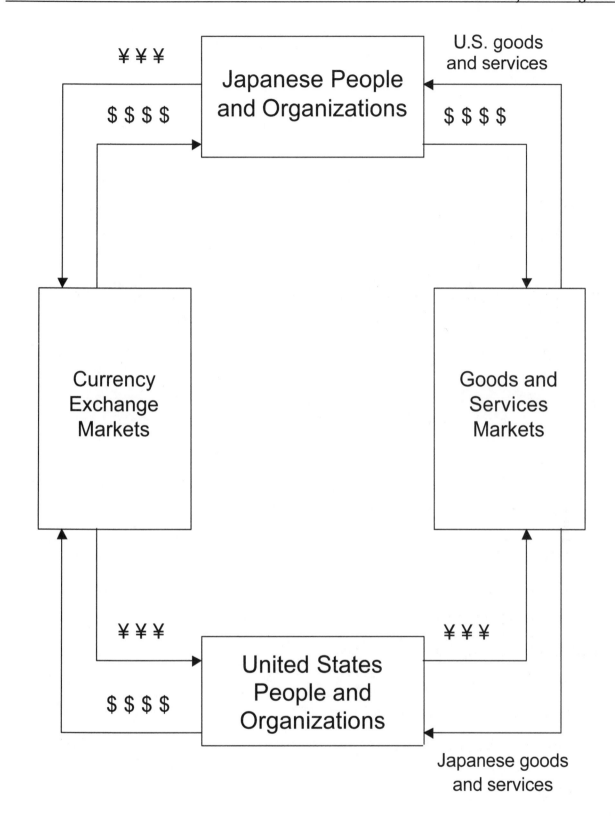